CONTEMPORARY SILVER
Made in Italy

CONTEMPORARY SILVER
Made in Italy

EVA CZERNIS-RYL

powerhouse publishing
part of the Powerhouse Museum

in association with

LUND HUMPHRIES

First published in 2004

Powerhouse Publishing, Sydney
PO Box K346 Haymarket NSW 1238
Australia

in association with

Lund Humphries
Gower House
Croft Road, Aldershot
Hampshire GU11 3HR
United Kingdom

Powerhouse Publishing is part of the Museum of Applied Arts and Sciences
www.powerhousemuseum.com/publish

Lund Humphries is part of Ashgate Publishing
www.lundhumphries.com

National Library of Australia CIP

Czernis-Ryl, Eva.
Contemporary silver: made in Italy.
Bibliography.
Includes index.
ISBN 1 86317 102 9 (pbk).
ISBN 0 85331 899 9 (hc).
1. Silverwork - Italy. I. Title.
739.230945

British Library Cataloguing-in-Publication Data
A catalogue record for this book is available from the British Library

ISBN 1 86317 102 9 (paperback edition)
ISBN 0 85331 899 9 (hardback edition)

Library of Congress Control Number: 2003114226

Contemporary silver: made in Italy © 2004 Museum of Applied Arts and Sciences (Powerhouse Museum), Sydney
Published in conjunction with the exhibition Contemporary silver: made in Italy at the Powerhouse Museum Aug 2004 – Feb 2005
Editing: Sue Wagner
Design: Peter Thorn, i2i design, Sydney
Project management: Julie Donaldson, Powerhouse Museum
Prepress: Spitting Image, Sydney
Printing: Produced through Phoenix Offset, printed in China

Distributed by Ashgate/Lund Humphries in all territories outside Australia and New Zealand (hardcover only).
Distributed in Australia and New Zealand by Bookwise International.

Frontispiece: 'Sole' (Sun) vase in sterling silver from the 'Minimal' collection, designed and made by Gabriele De Vecchi in 1992.

Collection: Museo per gli Argenti Contemporanei.
Photo courtesy of De Vecchi

Contents: detail from 'Quadro' vase (see plate 45).

Contents

Forewords

Contemporary silver: made in Italy has been published in association with the exhibition of the same name at the Powerhouse Museum. The exhibition celebrates the achievements of Italian silversmithing studios, architects and designers who have created contemporary silverware of distinction. Drawing predominantly on the collection of the Museo per gli Argenti Contemporanei, the exhibition is augmented by the iconic Tea & Coffee Piazzas from Alessi and the striking recent creations from the De Vecchi and San Lorenzo studios, Cleto Munari, Pampaloni and Sawaya & Moroni. Examples of Alessi's new Tea & Coffee Towers and some of the latest centrepieces designed by Ettore Sottsass Jr, complete the selection.

The Powerhouse Museum is delighted to present this exhibition which complements both the Museum's strong interest in design and its diverse collection which includes over 100 000 decorative arts and design objects.

Australia is home to a large number of people born in Italy or of Italian background. There is also a strong community of silversmiths whose highly individual work is marked by the quest for innovation and high standards. I am certain this exhibition will be well appreciated.

I am grateful to Dr Giorgio Forni, Manager of the Sartirana Art Foundation for making his collection available to us and also to Museo Alessi and other lenders for their generous loans. Finally, I wish to acknowledge Ilaria Cornaggia Medici Logi, for initiating the exhibition, and Eva Czernis-Ryl, curator of international decorative arts and design, for curating and coordinating the project, and the many Museum staff who have contributed to this handsome and scholarly publication and striking exhibition.

Dr Kevin Fewster AM
Director
Powerhouse Museum

Unlike Italy's historic castles which are renowned as showcases of old paintings and sculpture, the 14th century Castello of Sartirana in Lomellina, Lombardy, is the home to very different Italian treasures. A large part of its collection is modern. Developed since 1980 as part of the Lomellina Study Centre, and managed by the Sartirana Art Foundation from 1993, the collection is divided into six sections or museums: 20th-century silver and jewellery, textiles, dress, graphic art as well as glass, ceramics and furniture.

Comprising about 400 objects, the Museo per gli Argenti Contemporanei (MAC), was formally established in 1993 to record, stimulate and promote contemporary silverware made in Italy, particularly in Lombardy. With a strong focus on innovative design, the MAC has since assembled the largest and arguably the most important collection of silver made in Italy between the 1970s and today. While the core collection is concerned with the achievements of Milan's long-established, leading silversmithing firms such as De Vecchi and San Lorenzo, an increasing range of objects is also being acquired from other Italian studios which pursue excellence in contemporary silver design and production.

As the Foundation's aim is to make its collections widely accessible, a large part of the MAC holdings has traveled over the past decade to museums and galleries in many countries. This is the first time that the collection is shown in Australia and we are pleased indeed to be able to display it in Sydney's largest and most prestigious museum. I would like to express my gratitude to Dr Kevin Fewster and his staff for making this exhibition and publication possible.

Dr Giorgio Forni
Manager
Fondazione Sartirana Arte

Contemporary silver: made in Italy

Today, Italy is not only the world's leading producer of silver articles, manufacturing some 1600 metric tonnes in the year 2000, but also a powerhouse of innovative and forward looking ideas for silver design.[1] Developed alongside Italy's other decorative arts, such as furniture and ceramics, which were increasingly perceived as industrial products, silverware in the second half of the 20th century followed a path of its own. Traditionally crafted in small workshops and seen as incompatible with mass production, it remained in the shadow of the international success of Italian industrial design until the 1980s.

Ironically, the refusal to industrialise, the very thing that kept contemporary silverware in the background from the 1950s, was also responsible for its revival beginning in the 1970s. Small-scale workshops were more flexible than larger producers and were not afraid to experiment or bring stylistic innovation into their designs. They also tended to be less affected by economic crises some of which had disastrous consequences for larger industries. A key factor in the success of Italian silver, as in many other areas of Italian design, was cooperation with prominent architects, both Italian and international. While in England and other European countries, mid to late 20th-century silver was designed and made by trained silversmiths alone, the emergence of modern silverware in Italy was engineered by Italian silversmiths, producers and patrons working closely with talented architects. The introduction of serial production directed at niche markets, initiated in 1970 by the studio San Lorenzo, enabled a greater exposure and commercial rewards.

When discussing contemporary silver made in Italy, it is impossible not to mention the country's history of decorative precious metalwork which has contributed to its achievements. This history, however, also proved an enduring obstacle on silver's winding road to modernity.

A fabulous tradition: from antiquity to the early 20th century

Likened to the moon and used sparingly for small, often mystical objects, in earliest times silver was more scarce than gold.[2] Silversmithing on a larger scale was first practised in Mesopotamia when the gold and silver deposits of Anatolia (Turkey) became available from about 2500 BC. Silverware played an important role in ancient Greece, and during the Hellenistic times (c 330–50 BC) domestic silver and objects for personal use became common. Sacrificial bowls, drinking vessels and other objects have survived in burial places from early Etruria, now central Italy, especially from the 7th century BC.[3]

It was the Romans, however, who became the first and most enthusiastic collectors of silverware.[4] Vessels and utensils recovered from houses destroyed by the eruption of Vesuvius in AD 79, and in particular from household goods buried in times of strife, illustrate a fabulous range of designs

This cup and footed dish are electrotype reproductions of original objects from a magnificent hoard of Roman domestic silver excavated near Hildesheim in Germany in 1868. They were made by Elkington & Co, London, about 1883. Cup 35 cm (h), dish 8.5 cm (diam).

available in the early Roman Empire. New forms were developed in succeeding centuries, mainly in Rome, where silversmiths used a wide range of techniques: silver could be cast, hammered, chased, engraved, inlaid with gold and electrum, applied with high-relief medallions and decorated with gilt and niello, a decorative inlay of black metallic compound. Roman models strongly influenced early Byzantine silver and continue to inspire modern silversmiths in many parts of the world even today.

When Italy embraced the gothic style in the 13th century silversmithing flourished again, and in larger towns the trade was regulated by guilds. The 14th century was particularly rich in gold objects but marvellous ecclesiastical silver and domestic silverware were also crafted. Although medieval goldsmiths (silversmiths also made gold objects and were known as goldsmiths at the time) were held in high esteem, it was during the Italian renaissance in the late 15th century that

A view of a 17th-century silversmiths' workshop from *A touch-stone for gold and silver wares, or a manual for goldsmiths...* by William Badcock, London, 1677.

works in precious metals came to be considered an art form equal to painting and sculpture. The epoch's foremost architects and artists, including Filippo Brunelleschi and Lorenzo Ghiberti, also trained as goldsmiths. The skill of Italian goldsmiths was widely admired and some were lured to work at grand European courts. It was at the court of Francis I of France that the most famous work in precious metals of the time, the sculptural saliera or saltcellar, was made by the legendary Benvenuto Cellini in about 1540.

Italian mannerist silver of the mid 16th century was particularly inventive and showed the extraordinary technical virtuosity of its makers. Rome was the birthplace of Europe's most dramatic style, 17th century baroque, which also produced extravagant silver. Although France and Germany, mainly the city of Augsburg, took over as leaders in making fashionable silver in the following century, Italian rococo and neoclassical objects developed their own distinctive character.

Saliera or saltcellar in gold, enamels and ebony made by the Italian goldsmith Benvenuto Cellini for King Francis I in Paris between 1540 and 1543. Saltcellar 26 cm (h).
Photo courtesy of the Kunsthistorisches Museum, Vienna.

Vase of silver and gilt bronze made by Giovanni Bellezza (1807–76) in Milan in 1866. The design of this vase was inspired by the late renaissance style (mannerism) of the 16th century, Italy's golden epoch. The renaissance revival style was used by Italian silversmiths as a symbol of Italian national aspirations. Vase 41.7 cm (h).

Until the unification of Italy in 1870, the country was dominated by foreign powers. Most of northern Italy was under the rule of Austria, then briefly of Napoleon, only to be fragmented again at the Congress of Vienna in 1815. Struggle for independence and political unity marked much of the 19th century, during which silversmiths designed objects in styles borrowed from Italy's illustrious past. The most ambitious works were made in Rome, Naples, Milan, Vicenza and Genoa, and silversmiths such as Antonio Cortelezzo and Giovanni Bellezza achieved much acclaim. At the turn of the century Italy succumbed to the art nouveau style, creating its own version known as 'stile Liberty'. Pastiches of historical styles, however, continued to dominate local markets and it is these highly ornamental designs that Italy's futurist artists and rationalist architects of the 1920s and 1930s sought to bring more in line with international developments.

Towards modern silver: 1915 to the 1960s

The foundations for modern Italian silver were laid during World War I, when the Italian government excluded German businesses from the national market.[5] Most of those companies closed down, while some continued with Italian management, and new Italian firms were established. This patriotic measure, however, when combined with the effect of the greatly reduced number of international fairs in Italy meant that Italian design suffered for some years from a lack of exposure to contemporary developments in other countries.

 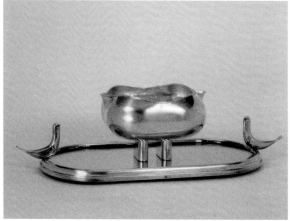

'Futurismo' silver and wood centrepiece from the 'Sant' Elia' series made by Arrigo Finzi in Milan about 1920. This is a rare example of silver design influenced by Italian futurism. The title of the series refers to the futurist architect Antonio Sant' Elia who is believed to have provided designs for silver to Finzi before he died in 1916.

Photo courtesy of Olga Finzi Baldi.

'Fontana' centrepiece from the 'Sant' Elia' series designed and made by Arrigo Finzi in Milan about 1934. A similar centrepiece by Finzi was awarded a prize at the Exposition Universelle et Internationale in Brussels in 1935. Centrepiece 14.5 cm (h).

Photo courtesy of Olga Finzi Baldi.

Benito Mussolini's fascist regime was keen to foster Italian art and industry. Beginning with the first Monza Biennale of Decorative Arts in 1923, the next two decades witnessed an unprecedented number of decorative arts and design shows.[6] Objects in silver and other materials were also sent to international exhibitions in Paris, Brussels and elsewhere, while in 1928 Domus, one of the first modern design magazines, was launched with the architect Gio Ponti as its editor. Rational modernism or rationalism, an architectural style which developed in Italy from the early 1920s, had little impact on silver design, and by 1936 it had lost its battle with the novecento style, which drew on both Italy's classical traditions and a modern aesthetic, as the national visual style. While Domus promoted the novecento style, with both French art deco and Austrian models of the Wiener Werkstätte presented as desirable sources of inspiration, the Milan Triennales served as the world's leading survey of international design and a prestigious showcase for local talent.[7] Acclaimed art historian Giulio Carlo Argan summarised their importance in 1972: 'Italian design developed in the display booths at fairs and expositions before finding a place in industrial ateliers'.[8]

The popularity of novecento, a style widely used in architecture, encouraged decorative arts manufacturers to engage architects as designers for their products. In the tradition of the great Italian architects of the renaissance and baroque periods, Carlo Scarpa designed Venini glass, Gio Ponti's ceramics contributed to the success of the Richard Ginori factory, and Ponti's and Ignazio Gardella's designs for silver secured their makers medals at the Monza Biennale in 1930 and the Milan Triennale in 1936. Distinctly modern in appearance, for the first time Italian silver tableware, cutlery, presentation and even ecclesiastical silver were either left undecorated or were embellished with only restrained decoration. The scene was set for post-war developments.

Precious metals were not among the materials used in the years immediately after World War II; it was left to silver substitutes such as aluminum, stainless steel and silver-plate to carry on the design legacy of pre-war novecento in domestic metalwork. Particularly interesting objects were created by the silversmith Piero De Vecchi whose strikingly simple aluminum and silver-plated wares won awards at Milan's Triennale of the Reconstruction in 1947. De Vecchi's aluminum thermos was acquired by the Museum of Modern Art in New York. His timeless 'T8' candlestick, first made in electroplated silver, can be still bought today made in sterling silver.

When silver became available again in the late 1940s, its stylistic development was affected by a shift in Italian politics which brought a new design ideology.[9] The architecture-led rationalist aesthetic, which was revived immediately after the war, lost its case again, this time to post-war modernism which looked to contemporary abstract sculpture for inspiration. An international style which shaped much of the decorative arts in the 1950s, in Italy it lasted until the mid 1960s. It coincided with and gave visual expression to a period of accelerated industrial development, unprecedented

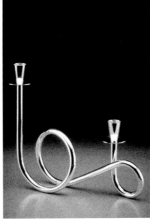

economic prosperity and remarkable inventiveness. Italy became the seventh industrial country in the world.[10] The success of the Italian furniture industry is well documented.[11] Italian glass and ceramics were also in great demand, and objects such Venini's 'Fasoletto' (Handkerchief) vase designed by Fulvio Bianconi and ceramics decorated with designs by Piero Fornasetti were to become icons of the era.[12]

The creativity of Italian designers and makers of the 1950s was not, however, limited to objects produced in these materials. Facilitated by low costs for both material and labour, silver also responded to the new stylistic stimuli — although historical styles still greatly outnumbered the new. The best objects continued to be recognised by awards at the Milan Triennales and also at the Compasso d'Oro (the Golden Compass awards).[13] The leading silversmiths of the 1950s were located in Milan and included the futurist artist Piero De Vecchi, Eros and Luigi Genazzi and Arrigo Finzi who designed and made highly individual tableware and presentation silver. A superb example is the tea service designed by Gio Ponti for Calderoni Gioielli and made by De Vecchi in 1956. Finzi's daughter, Olga Finzi Baldi, also made a significant contribution as evidenced by her ingenious stackable tea and coffee set 'Manhattan' (plate 1). Crafted in small numbers and confined to the local market, innovative Italian silverware was overshadowed by its well-marketed Scandinavian equivalents as well as by Italy's own spectacularly successful industrial design which, by the end of the decade, had become 'hot' in Europe.

One Italian metalworker, however, achieved international fame in the 1950s. An admirer of Gio Ponti, Lino Sabattini owed his success not only to his strikingly modern designs but also to the scale and production methods he used. Sabattini worked in silver-plated brass alloy rather than in sterling silver, using industrial methods, and his objects were intended for wide distribution at competitive prices.[14] While in the rest of Europe, particularly in Scandinavia, mass production of well-designed electroplated silver articles was seen as a viable and indeed commercially attractive option for silverware producers, Sabattini had a limited following in Italy. The strong silversmithing craft tradition, and customers' expectations that silver objects must be made by hand, ensured that Italian silver of the 1960s still came from traditional workshops. And since respect for traditional skills was closely associated with that for Italian heritage, this meant a strong preference for revivalist styles. 'Such is our romantic nostalgia today that we always imagine gold and silver treasures to have been made only in the past ...' wrote Graham Hughes in 1967.[15] This patronising of new silver 'antiques' was particularly evident in Italy.

As mainstream Italian industrial design departed from tradition, with outrageously coloured plastic furniture and kitchenware embraced enthusiastically by a new generation of consumers, the prospect for silver to be widely seen as a modern material declined. The flamboyant decade of the

Tea and coffee service designed by Gio Ponti for Calderoni Gioielli and made by Luigi Genazzi in 1930. Awarded a gold medal at the 4th Monza Biennale.

Photo courtesy of Archivo Edografico Foundation La Triennale di Milano.

'T8' candlestick designed and made by Piero De Vecchi in Milan. Awarded a certificate of honour at the 8th Milan Triennale in 1947. Initially made in electroplated silver, it is available today made in sterling silver. Candlestick 25 cm (h).

Photo courtesy of the Museo per gli Argenti Contemporanei (MAC).

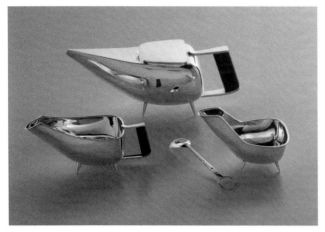 

Tea and coffee service designed by Gio Ponti for Calderoni Gioielli and made by Piero De Vecchi in Milan in 1956. Each piece in the set was made from a single sheet of silver.

Photo courtesy of De Vecchi.

Five production stages of a hand-hammered 'Elite' spoon (see plate 2).

Photo by Benedetta Calzavara, Powerhouse Museum.

1960s was youth-oriented, anti-establishment and anti-elitist. As the embodiment of an expensive, 'aristocratic' material, silver could not compete with the wide-spread appeal of new-age materials. Lack of adequate support from government or industry promotional bodies,[16] which played such an important role in the success of Scandinavian and English silver respectively, further ensured that the Italian silverware of the 1960s failed to capture the mood of the period and disappeared from view.

New visions, new challenges: the 1970s

While silver the material was not in favour in the 1960s, it was the colour of the era that brought dreams of space travel and the reality of the moon landing in 1969. Like spaceships, silvery metals (polished steel and aluminium) captured the imagination of the young; large modern silver rings were chic. For those who were concerned with the lack of availability of contemporary silverware, the increasing interest in 'silver' clearly presented a potential market. The 1970s looked promising for silver manufacturers as, despite economic recession, consumerism grew rapidly in Italy. Silver was still relatively inexpensive. The cost of labour, while much higher than in the 1950s, was not excessive, and at the time it approached that of silver in the total value of an object. Finally, the oil crisis of 1973 had aggravated Italy's economic instability and, aided by environmental concerns, severely affected the thriving plastics industry. Optimism was replaced by conservatism, and the fascination with plastics was replaced by an interest in more traditional and durable materials and in the crafts in general. Significantly, the economic crisis had little impact on small silversmithing firms and this fact further encouraged two forward-looking entrepreneurs who had recently decided to seize the opportunity.

When in 1962 Gabriele De Vecchi succeeded his father Piero in their Milan family business Argenteria De Vecchi, which was established in 1935, he 'hated it passionately'.[17] Although the firm's silverware was regularly exhibited in the Milan Triennales, commercially it was difficult to keep the spirit of modern silver alive in the Italy of the 1960s. A founding member of 'Gruppo T' (1959–63), he devoted most of his time to artistic activities relating to kinetic art.[18] At that stage, De Vecchi's artistic pursuits had little influence on his designs for silverware.

In 1970, however, De Vecchi began revising his approach to silver design and production. 'I realised that I was producing forms that could be made in any material,' he recalls.[19] This was when he became fascinated both with silver's unmatched ability to reflect light and with the idea of silver as a mirror. De Vecchi observed that while polished gold produces a yellow shadow, and steel tints its shadow blue, polished silver reflects up to 98 percent of light. Because it is so reflective, it cannot be cut by laser.[20] He also experimented with the interactive qualities of silver. Smooth, polished silver

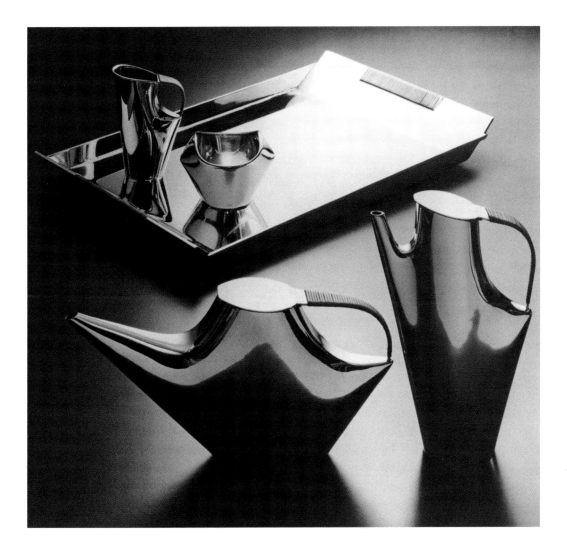

Tea and coffee service 'Como' designed by Lino Sabattini in Milan in 1957 and made in silverplated brass by l'Orfévrerie Christofle in Paris. It illustrates particularly well the sensual forms and long flowing lines typical of 1950s modernism. Versions in sterling silver were also offered.

Photo courtesy of Lino Sabattini.

objects reflect their surroundings and merge with them, with outlines becoming ambiguous, changing and difficult for the eye to resolve. Keen to investigate the dynamics of these optical illusions, De Vecchi began to focus on the interplay of real and virtual forms and images in his works. With his aesthetic philosophy in place, De Vecchi was also keen to reduce the price of his objects while maintaining the high quality for which his firm was renowned. He introduced batch production, where objects were spun on lathes and formed in dies, the latter preferably designed as reusable modules suitable for more than one object. With this approach, the production process still involved extensive manual labour, but objects could be produced in multiples and in a much shorter time. With smooth, highly reflective surfaces crucial to each item's success, De Vecchi used rubber-die forming, a technique used in the aircraft industry and also responsible for the sleek body of the famous Vespa scooter.

Late in 1970 and in 1971, Argenteria De Vecchi released its first collections of sterling silver tableware, candlesticks and even a table lamp from the 'Arganto' and 'New Form' lines designed in collaboration with the architect Corinna Morandi (plate 4). These were followed by the 'Minimal' line designed by De Vecchi (plates 5, 6). Glossy brochures introduced the public to simple yet attractive designs. To diversify the plain surfaces of the new ranges, in 1973 the 'Gradini' line of stepped conical vases was introduced, all products of a single die, the resulting shapes cut and reassembled to make a range of forms. The late 1970s also saw the introduction of vases shaped as stylised female heads, beginning with 'Phoemina' (plate 7). These vases, as well as later objects from the 'Minimal' series, were to remain in De Vecchi's repertoire well into the 1990s. Very different from

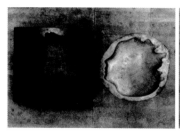  

Making the 'Phoemina' vase using
the die-stamping technique
(see plate 7).

Photo courtesy of De Vecchi.

a stylistic point of view, they heralded De Vecchi's intention to embrace disparate aesthetics while experimenting with light reflection and the sensual appeal of silver, an approach still evident in his work.

Determined to develop a formula for contemporary domestic silver, Milan-based Ciro Cacchione left his family's silversmithing business and, with his friends Antonio and Domenico Piva and Enrico Salvi, founded the studio San Lorenzo at the beginning of 1970.[21] A vigorous advocate of the idea that objects must be designed to reflect their own time, Cacchione assembled a permanent team of noted architects to create designs for his products. This novel approach was to bring outstanding results, and eventually San Lorenzo was honoured by an exhibition at the Victoria and Albert Museum in London.[22] Working closely with Cacchione and his silversmiths, the architect-designers aimed to define a new visual language for domestic silverware which would be modern, attractive, well made by a combination of traditional and industrial methods and, above all highly usable. Antonio Piva, Franco Albini and Franca Helg, Afra and Tobia Scarpa, Massimo and Lella Vignelli and Maria Luisa Belgiojoso were initially to design specific groups of objects, for example Albini and Helg were to be responsible for tea and coffee sets, Belgiojoso for objects for children and the Scarpas for writing sets.[23] However, in order to encourage a greater interest in objects designed in the modern idiom in a very traditional market, the earliest range was mainly restricted to tableware and cutlery, the most popular silver articles used in Italian homes (plates 8–13).[24]

Brochure for Argenteria De Vecchi's
'Arganto' collection, 1970.

Photo courtesy of De Vecchi.

Gabriele De Vecchi (b 1938) art
director of the De Vecchi studio
in Milan.

Photo by Maria Mulas, courtesy of De Vecchi.

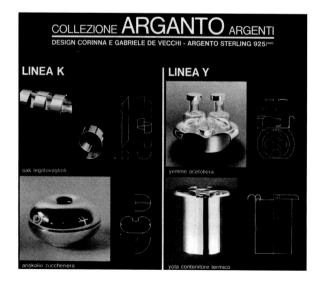 

Launched in 1970, San Lorenzo's inaugural collection demonstrated confident designs, which focused on the sensitive use of material, while representing a restrained modernist aesthetic. The extensive range of tableware designed by Antonio Piva, the renowned architect and professor at the Milan Polytechnic, is a splendid example (plate 8). The classical monumentality of Piva's tea and coffee pots is played down by fine silver-wire handles and frosted-glass bodies of carafes, bowls and oil and vinegar containers. As opposed to Gabriele De Vecchi's devotion to unembellished surfaces, from the beginning San Lorenzo objects offered a variety of finishes. The eye-catching 'Pannocchia' bowls, designed by Albini and Helg, rely for their effect on the traditional repoussé technique: the cob-like pattern decorating the surface of the bowls is meticulously hammered by hand, with the largest bowl requiring 25 000 individual 'kernels' to complete the design (plate 10).[25] From the finely striated surfaces of the Vignellis' glamorous bar set (plate 11) to the Scarpas' ingenious 'cardboard' boxes (plate 12) and brilliantly designed polygonal vases (plate 13), the San Lorenzo collection abounded in creative solutions. Objects were displayed in a purpose-designed showroom and could be purchased from San Lorenzo's first retail shop located in Milan's prestigious via Santo Spirito. Attractive packaging, a comprehensive catalogue and a promotional film completed the portfolio. San Lorenzo's range generated excellent reviews and was recognised, in both the local and the international press, as the first truly modern collection of domestic silverware and a model for younger silversmiths to follow.[26] Also well received by the public, San Lorenzo objects were to significantly influence stylistic developments in both silver and stainless steel tableware in Italy for years to come.

This flurry of activity in the two Milanese studios must have not escaped the attention of Cleto Munari, a self-confessed 'dandy' turned key patron and collector of contemporary Italian silver.[27] Based in Vicenza in north-eastern Italy, Munari was neither a silversmith nor a silverware manufacturer and his vision for late 20th-century silver was not to be compromised by the moods and demands of the market. With a keen interest in design, and being a friend of some of the leading Italian architects, he set out to explore the possibilities of silver as a modern medium. To realise his ambition, he resolved to collaborate with distinguished architects, by now an established Italian formula for successful product design.

In the mid 1970s Munari approached the Venetian architect Carlo Scarpa to design cutlery for him. The result was a set of light and exquisitely balanced spoons, forks and knives designed in 1977 (plate 15). Several other pieces soon followed including an unusual octagonal vase, a fruit tray and a jug with gilded interior (also plate 15). Collaboration with Scarpa was crucial to Munari as a patron and collector. It not only started his remarkable collection but also established his role as a catalyst in the designs of his objects, from the initial idea to the final stages of production. With time Munari would acquire more confidence and design objects himself. 'Scarpa had an immense

Above, l-r: Ciro Cacchione (b 1942), founding director of the studio San Lorenzo in Milan.

Franca Helg (1929–89) and Franco Albini (1905–77) began working together in 1952. Albini's sparse designs for architecture and objects had been formulated before World War II under the influence of modernism. Albini and Helg continued this restrained approach in their designs for San Lorenzo.

Maria Luisa Belgiojoso graduated from Milan Polytechnic in 1964. Assistant to Aldo Rossi from 1965 to 1967, she later worked for her architect father, Lodovico Belgiojoso; since 1981 she has worked from her own office in Milan.

Antonio Piva (b 1936) is professor of architecture at Milan Polytechnic; he also lectures in Brazil and Greece, is a UNESCO adviser and a Milan-based architect and designer.

Tobia and Afra Scarpa trained as architects at Venice University, they have been working together since 1957. The Scarpas are widely acknowledged for their sensitive use of materials and for the longevity of their designs.

Lella and Massimo Vignelli were educated in Venice, Cambridge (UK) and Milan as architects and designers. They have worked together since 1960. Their furniture and product design have brought them many prestigious awards.

Photos courtesy of San Lorenzo.

Cleto Munari, Carlo Scarpa and Ettore Sottsass Jr in the 1970s.
Photo courtesy of Cleto Munari Design Associati.

San Lorenzo's first shop, designed by Antonio Piva, in Milan's via Santo Spirito. Photo courtesy of San Lorenzo.

Page from San Lorenzo's first catalogue illustrated with photographs by Aldo Ballo, 1970.
Photo courtesy of San Lorenzo.

prestige ... nobody refused to work with me,' he laughs when talking about subsequent designers he approached during this formative period for his collection.[28] Munari worked at the time with Achille Castiglioni, Gae Aulenti, Alessandro Mendini, Mario Bellini, Vico Magistretti and Ettore Sottsass Jr (plate 16), all highly respected architects. Keen to view Italian developments in a wider context, Munari also travelled extensively, meeting and befriending international architects; the Viennese architect Hans Hollein became his first international designer. While these architects designed sophisticated silver objects worthy of a most discerning contemporary consumer, it was Michele De Lucchi's covered jug commissioned by Munari which revealed an entirely new direction in design for domestic silver (plate 17). Resembling more a cartoon character than a silver vessel, its long, cylindrical silver body sported yellow conical feet, a baby-blue industrial-style handle and a pink finial. With these details provocatively made of plastic, the jug spelled a breakthrough for silverware design. Finely crafted by Rossi & Arcandi, a Vicenza firm of highly skilled silversmiths established in 1959, Cleto Munari's objects more than fulfilled his vision for outstanding silver tableware: they pushed the boundaries of silver design.

The golden decade: 1980s

Mostly as a result of the efforts of the San Lorenzo and De Vecchi studios and later Cleto Munari, Italian silverware became increasingly visible during the 1970s. Its design embraced diversely individual styles in contrast to the unified aesthetic of the modernism of the 1950s, inspired by organic sculpture. By the 1980s, through association with some of Italy's most creative architect-designers, silverware had found itself at the centre of the second wave of the anti-design movement which rejected all forms of modernism including the current 'good taste' of many Italian products. In particular, the movement was opposed to the idea of design as a tool of industry, for creating objects as status symbols rather than to enhance the domestic environment.

Most of the leading figures of this movement, including Mendini, Sottsass, Andrea Branzi and De Lucchi, were centred around Studio Alchimia, founded in 1976 in Milan, and by now the undisputed centre of contemporary design. When De Lucchi designed his playful jug for Cleto Munari in 1979, he, like the others, was searching for ways to revitalise Italian design by reconnecting it with everyday life and culture. Symbols and colours from popular culture, humour and distorted scale and form were among the sources that inspired his designs. Among Studio Alchimia's prototypes was a group of electrical appliances designed by De Lucchi and displayed in the 16th Milan Triennale in 1979. The unmistakable pastel colours and toy-like shapes of these objects reveal the origins of the Munari jug, arguably the earliest example of multi-coloured, mixed-media radical design to be proposed for Italian domestic silver.

Members of the Memphis group photographed in 1981 in the 'Tawaraya' boxing ring designed by Masanori Umeda. From left: Aldo Cibic, Andrea Branzi, Michele De Lucchi, Marco Zanini, Natalie Du Pasquier, George J Sowden, Martine Bedin, Matteo Thun and Ettore Sottsass.

Photo courtesy of Memphis SRL, Milan.

Studio Alchimia was the forerunner of Memphis, a design cooperative set up by Sottsass in the winter of 1980-81. With an international outlook and a view to the mainstream, Memphis designers were keen to utilise commercial opportunities in contrast with Alchimia's more research-oriented and intellectual bias. The former Alchimia members Sottsass and De Lucchi were joined by Barbara Radice, Marco Zanini, Aldo Cibic, Matteo Thun, Martine Bedin, George Sowden, Natalie Du Pasquier and several international architects including Hans Hollein. Alongside their best known and hugely influential products such as furniture, fabrics, lighting and ceramics, the group produced a range of innovative blown-glass objects and extraordinary silverware (plates 18–23).

These models for electrical appliances in painted wood, influenced the design of the De Lucchi's silver jug (see plate 17). They were designed by Michele De Lucchi for Girmi and displayed in the 16th Milan Triennale in 1979.

Photo courtesy of Michele De Lucchi.

Crafted by Rossi & Arcandi, silver objects designed by Sottsass, Branzi, Du Pasquier, and 'guest' designers Peter Shire and Daniela Puppa, formed part of the 1982 Memphis collection. With the exception of glassware (which was hand-blown on Murano, near Venice) all objects were intended for unlimited production, and silver designs were also available in electroplated silver.

Although the colourful details of De Lucchi's jug suggested the beginning of colour infusion into silver, Memphis silverware remained largely monochromatic with only occasional accents of colour, pattern or different materials. One of the reasons for this was the fact that even Memphis had to comply with centuries-old regulations which protect the lawful quality of the precious metal, and forbid debasing it with other materials.[29]

It was therefore not so much colour or pattern but rather the fantastic forms that carried the Memphis message by defying the basic notion of functionalism and refusing to follow function. In Memphis's small silver world, the serving tray resembled a miniature bed, the fruit bowl looked like a deck chair and a sauceboat assumed the shape of a surreal ice-cream cone held in place by a branch-like handle (plates 20 & 22). Interestingly, though, this world remained true to its material and indeed it revelled in it. Drawing attention to the cold, shiny surface of the metal, the names given to objects such as 'Antarctic', 'Alaska' or 'Labrador' evoke frigid climates to further seduce their users. This emphasis on the sensual qualities of silver, as well as on image, combined with

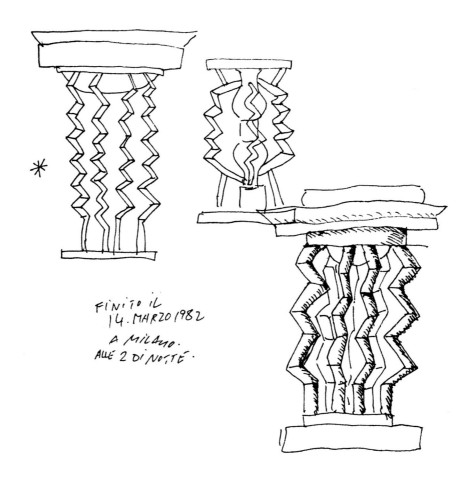

FINITO IL
14. MARZO 1982
A MILANO.
ALLE 2 DI NOTTE.

Ettore Sottsass' design drawings for the centrepiece 'Murmansk' by Memphis, 1982 (see plate 23).

Photo courtesy of Memphis SRL, Milan.

Memphis's usual decontextualising of materials, explains why these advocates of banal, tasteless and 'uncultured' materials, epitomised by plastic laminates, would take an interest in silver. As Barbara Radice pointed out: 'Moving in this freedom-giving context, which appeals more to physical qualities than to the intellect, Memphis designers have even succeeded in revitalising cultivated, traditional and familiar materials ... used in irreverent forms that do not correspond to recognised uses of the material.'[30]

This postmodern sensibility, and in particular the idea that design should incorporate symbolic messages and take into account the emotional responses of consumers, also guided concurrent developments at Alessi, Italy's leading decorative metalwork manufacturer based in Crusinallo in northern Italy. Founded in 1921 by Giovanni Alessi Anghini, in 1955 the company began collaborating with outside designers on their predominantly stainless steel tableware. From the early 1970s, on the initiative of Alberto Alessi, who has just joined the firm of his father Carlo (Giovanni's son), it enlisted the services of its first architect, Ettore Sottsass Jr. Soon cooperation also began with the German-born architect Richard Sapper and later with Achille Castiglioni. In 1979 Alessandro Mendini joined Alessi as a design consultant.

Intending to renew the company's profile and to expand markets, Alessandro Mendini and Alberto Alessi devised a plan for a new project, 'Programma 6', in 1979–80. Its aim was to foster research and experimentation that included the use of new materials and production processes. The chosen theme was the tea and coffee service, a classic Alessi product. Acknowledging the key role of architects in the success of 20th-century Italian design, they approached a group of leading Italian and international architects to each design a tea and coffee set. The architects were asked to reassess the very concept of the familiar tableware with a long history of production and use, and consider

Alberto Alessi (b 1953) in 1996. The teapot is a reinterpretation of the 'Bombé' teapot designed by his father Carlo Alessi.

its relationship with contemporary architecture. In addition to Mendini, ten architects were selected to work on the project: Michael Graves (USA), Hans Hollein (Austria), Charles Jencks (USA/Britain), Richard Meier (USA), Stanley Tigerman (USA), Oscar Tusquets (Spain) Robert Venturi (USA), Kazumasa Yamashita (Japan) and two Italians, Paolo Portoghesi and Aldo Rossi. While initially all participants intended to provide designs for industrial production, the sets proved too complex for a serial approach and eventually most pieces were hand crafted in sterling silver. Only 99 copies of each set were to be made.

Released under the auspices of Officina Alessi, the company's new studio for experimental projects, the 'Tea & Coffee Piazza' series was launched in October 1983 in Milan and New York. Geometric or organic, minimalist or surreal, each set in the series was remarkable for its originality and flair. They were also very different from each other, as could be expected from exponents of postmodernism, an eclectic style that drew on a vast range of references including historical styles, particularly classical, a mix of the highbrow and the populist, the lighthearted, the metaphorical, as well as exploring decoration, colour and texture (plates 24–34).

Most services in this diverse group drew on architectural forms, and indeed those with the strongest architectural content tended to receive the greatest attention from both critics and consumers. From Michael Graves's squat, massive 'buildings' wrapped around with shimmering colonnades surmounted with blue-enamelled balls, to Jencks's disintegrating columns in postmodern ionic order, to Rossi's anthropomorphic towers performing secret rituals behind the glass doors of a teatrino scientifico, these sets also had stories to tell. This is how Charles Jencks interpreted the Mendini service when he first saw it in a 1981 preview: 'the pert little birds — the shiny round globes with tubes — look, perhaps, less like fat aviary creatures than some high-gloss, high-tech,

underwater bombs' (plate 34).[31] The series was a triumph. It generated much publicity, including a touring exhibition in the USA, and brought Alessi international recognition. Silver as a material for tableware was benefiting greatly from the exposure.

Just as Memphis prompted a wave of formal experiments in design studios and silversmiths' workshops the world over, Alessi's objects demonstrated that imaginatively designed silver tableware could be both ground breaking in design and attractive to the public. Acknowledging that the sets were priced beyond the means of most consumers, the ideas developed for the series were used to design commercial 'offshoots' in stainless steel. Consequently, while design museums and private collectors vied with each other to acquire the silver piazzas, Aldo Rossi's 1984 'La Conica' coffeemaker and Michael Graves's 'Kettle with a bird-shaped whistle' of 1985 became international best-sellers, particularly among the growing class of young, successful professionals who bestowed on them a cult status. The series not only facilitated new opportunities for Alessi. It also had a

Design drawing for the
'Tea & Coffee Piazza' by Mendini
(see plate 34).

profound impact on the appearance of domestic tableware, in silver, stainless steel and other materials and, as Philippa Glanville noted, it redefined the public perception of modernism itself.[32] Richard Meier, the designer of one of the more complex piazzas, wrote about the project in 1996: 'With great innovation and creativity the Alessi company has introduced a line of products which have a great appeal not only to design conscious consumers but to the general public whose awareness of quality motivates their purchases. Alessi has been responsible for elevating the general level of design around the world by serving as an inspiration for other design companies to create objects of distinction ...'.[33] By that time, the photogenic services from the 'Tea & Coffee Piazza' series had already been illustrated in design history books where, alongside outrageous furniture by Memphis, they had featured as icons of postmodernism.

While the best publicised and most witty 'designer' objects of the decade were assuming the role of status symbols during the 1980s (the very notion that the anti-design movement opposed in the

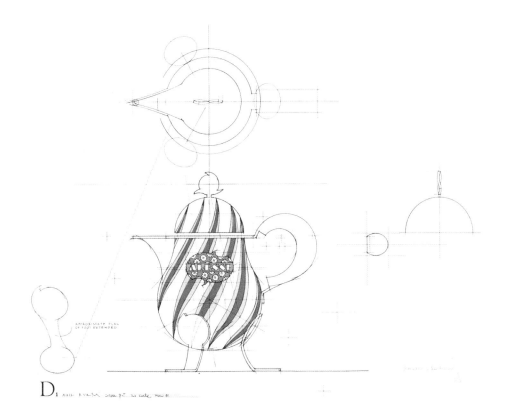

Design drawing for a coffeepot from 'Tea & Coffee Piazza' by Robert Venturi (see plate 31).

Collection: Museo Alessi. Photo courtesy of Alessi.

Aldo Rossi's architectural model 'Il teatrino scientifico' of 1978, which inspired the design for his 'Tea & Coffee Piazza' (see plate 24).

1970s), their creators were hailed as 'stars'. Through his contacts with many leading designers, Cleto Munari witnessed the evolution of the design-led culture at first hand — his own objects were conceived by some of the best-known architects as early as the 1970s. It is interesting to note that several of his architect-designed silver tea and coffee sets, as well as those made earlier by San Lorenzo, predate Alessi's project (plates 8, 9, 16). Munari expanded his collection throughout the decade and many of his post-1983 objects show the combined Memphis-Alessi influence. More expressive and less serious, they include the 'Pinguino' (Penguin) service by Memphis's Matteo Thun (plate 35) and Mendini's playful candlesticks (plate 36), distant cousins of his 'Tea & Coffee Piazza'.[34] Other additions to the collection during this period included sculptural vases by Angelo Mangiarotti (plate 37), vessels by Roberto Sambonet and Giotto Stoppino (plate 38), cutlery by Paolo Portoghesi and jugs by Mario Botta (plate 39). Well-travelled and published and shown in prestiguous museums, objects in the Munari collection remained virtually unique, with occasional copies made for museums and individual fans.[35]

As far as the production of objects in silver for the general and niche markets was concerned, however, it was left to small, specialist silversmithing firms to meet the demand for more affordable objects. Despite Italian economic, political and cultural insecurities, the 1980s witnessed a rapidly growing consumerism which generated the desire for an increasing number of visually appealing objects by ever more affluent consumers.

Within the atmosphere of rejoicing in stylistic freedom, Gabriele De Vecchi, by now also a trained architect, continued his experiments with the impact of light reflection on silver design. In 1981–82 he introduced two distinctive lines. 'Speriment' (Experiment) focused on self-reflection or the effect that various 'broken', superimposed or interestingly juxtaposed surfaces can have on each other and therefore on the appearance of the object (plates 40–42). For the 'Storia' (History) line (plates 43, 44), he made highly ornamental, 18th-century style jugs, candlesticks and tankards that had parts 'sliced off' to achieve clean contrasting surfaces. Sometimes a sharp triangular wedge would split a coffeepot or act as a suprematist spout to bring the form of the vessel into the modern era. 'Hybridisation,' De Vecchi notes, 'helps to dispel a certain aura around objects made of silver'.[36] Among his most unusual objects is the 'vanishing' 'Torincubo' teapot from the 'Storia' range. While the plain surfaces at the bottom merge with their surroundings to virtually disappear from view, the ornate top part of the vessel seems to be left suspended in the air (plate 43; see also frontispiece). As with his earlier 'Minimal' series, the challenges posed by these two lines would continue to occupy De Vecchi and mesmerise his clients throughout the 1990s.

San Lorenzo and its pioneering team of architect-designers continued to produce exquisitely designed objects in the 1980s, each piece finely crafted to suit its specific function and satisfy our senses. Among San Lorenzo's new products at the time, two series deserve particular attention. The 'Guillochis' boxes designed by Maria Luisa Belgiojoso are decorated in an 18th-century technique of bright-cut engraving where patterns of lined triangles create stunning graphic effects through the play of light moving along the grooved lines in different directions (plate 47). But it is the 'Moretta' jugs and bowls, designed by Afra and Tobia Scarpa at the turn of the decade, that reveal the essence of San Lorenzo's approach (plate 48). Fitting snugly into the hand, exquisitely balanced and pouring flawlessly, they are a tribute to the Scarpas' remarkable ability to transform ordinary articles into distinctively modern objects which are a delight to handle and to use.[37]

The growing number of exhibitions, regular press reviews and keen interest from museums, as well as the prestige that came from such exposure, prompted the expansion of other businesses, many keen to supplement their traditional lines with 'designer' silverware. Tea and coffee services issued by Pomellato from Venice and Pampaloni from Florence (plates 49 & 50) are among the most delightful items of tableware made in the later 1980s. Even firms which until now were only interested in other materials, such as Danese from Milan, were keen to offer state-of-the-art silverware to their clients, produced in series according to demand. In 1984 Verona's Fratelli Filippini, a luxury glass and leather objects manufacturer, set up Gemma Gioielli, a new division intended to make artist jewellery. By 1990 they had begun producing silver hollowware designed by the Milanese architect-designer Claudio Salocchi. The Salocchi collection of sleek and unpretentious bar accessories was completed in 1992 (plates 51–53). Olga Finzi Baldi's one-off objects were exclusively designed and crafted by her directly for individual clients (plate 54).

Olga Finzi Baldi with 'Giano' jug and other objects she designed, in her Milanese studio, 2003.

Photo by Benedetta Calzavara, Powerhouse Museum.

Looking to the future: 1990s and beyond

During the 1970s and in particular throughout the affluent 1980s, Italian silver was transformed from a largely conservative material, deeply rooted in history, into a modern medium capable of exciting the greatest designers and most prestigious decorative arts and design museums. This metamorphosis continued to evolve as the new decade unfolded.

Responding to their customers' unceasing demand for 'signature' pieces, silversmithing firms and design companies continued to engage noted architects and designers as creators of their silver products. Milan's Sawaya & Moroni, a furniture and accessories manufacturer founded in 1984, responded to the challenge particularly seriously. In 1991 the firm established a specialist silversmithing workshop. In addition to using the talents of its own William Sawaya (plate 55), the firm began commissioning silver designs from some of the most outstanding European architects and designers, who also provided designs for their furniture collection. Among their 'stars' were the French architect Jean Nouvel and Zaha Hadid, the London-based, Iraqi-born architect renowned for her amazing deconstructivist designs. While Nouvel's design for his champagne bucket (plate 57) demonstrates a classically elegant approach, Hadid's tea and coffee set, almost threatening in appearance particularly when assembled for storage as a sharp-angled structure, is arguably the most expressive example of the 1990s micro architecture for the table (plate 58).

From the late 1990s, Pampaloni, a century-old Florentine firm of manufacturing silversmiths, also assembled an impressive pool of architects, designers and artists to develop the 'Evasioni' and 'Evoluzioni' lines which parallel their varied historical collections (plates 59, 60). From Lapo Binazzi to Ettore Sottsass Jr, from Nigel Coates to Mario Mariotti, the firm's sumptuous, glossy catalogues list nearly 50 guest designers carefully selected to appeal to local and international markets.

While continuing to extend and refine his 'Speriment', 'Storia' and 'Minimal' series (plate 61), Gabriele De Vecchi also maintained close working relationships with architect-designers throughout the 1990s. Although this resulted in 'Maduar', a commercial line of domestic articles designed by Maurizio Duranti, De Vecchi's reasons were not only market driven: he saw these 'encounters' as a form of enrichment which also facilitated an exchange of ideas.[38] In 1991, for example, he launched a series of objects designed by Ugo La Pietra (plates 62, 63) whose objects called for a very different approach to design and production processes and put De Vecchi's skills as a craftsman to a 'harsh test'.[39]

The silversmith Carlo Vallé of Argenteria M Vallé, established in 1931, at work in his Milanese workshop in 2003.

Photo by Benedetta Calzavara with kind permission of Vallé Mario SNC.

In 1993, a different form of enrichment, this time of the entire picture of contemporary silver in Lombardy, was being orchestrated by the new Museo per gli Argenti Contemporanei (MAC) in Sartirana Lomellina, Pavia, in northern Italy. While the museum began collecting silverware to document developments predominantly of the last three decades, they were also aware of a limited interest in this area. In order to stimulate the commitment of silversmiths to modern silver, they invited twelve Italian designers and as many firms willing to produce their designs. Although the resulting MAC Collection '93 (plates 66–70) did not survive beyond the prototype stage, with objects made by the firms Mazzucato and Vallé as exceptions, the experiment had a considerable impact on the trade which is still in evidence today. This was a significant achievement especially since the economic climate of the early 1990s called for profitability and new designs were risky. The prosperity of those studios which concentrated exclusively on contemporary designs, however, had to be achieved by different means. 'The years of poetry were over,' recalls Cleto Munari when explaining his transformation from a private collector of unique items to a businessman with an international multi-media company with its own workshop in Vicenza and factory in Padova in north-east Italy.[40] Although still expanding his spectacular silver collection, from the early 1990s Munari has focused on silverware and accessories produced in large numbers and intended for sale. Soon other firms were also busy implementing larger production runs, creating new 'brands' with catalogues both printed and accessible online. With a new millennium on the horizon, this was also

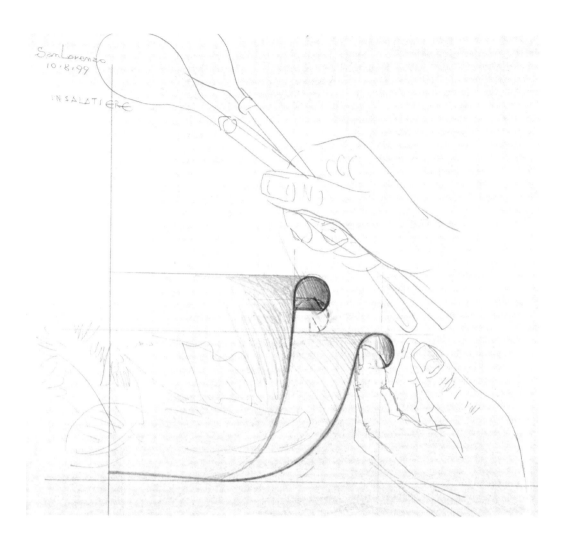

Tobia Scarpa's design drawing for a pure (999) silver risotto pot (see plate 74).

Photo courtesy of San Lorenzo.

a good opportunity to reassess their products, and in particular the products' relevance to users, now and in the future.

This is when San Lorenzo's Ciro Cacchione turned his attention to silver as a material for cooking wares. While researching, in collaboration with Milan Polytechnic, the best silver alloy for such objects, Cacchione discovered not only that pure silver (999 parts of silver mixed with one part of copper) was the best heat conductor of all metals but also that, contrary to the traditional belief, it could be worked on its own relatively easily. If you add to these findings the antiseptic, insoluble (non-reactive) and dishwasher-friendly properties of pure silver pots and pans, their reduced susceptibility to tarnish and the beautiful matt colour that is acquired with use, it is easy to understand why San Lorenzo has declared pure silver its material of the future. The 'Cooking in pure silver' range (plate 74) is ideal for cooking at lower temperatures, as the heat is spread evenly, a process which not only preserves nutrients and enhances flavours but also saves energy. Carefully designed by Afra and Tobia Scarpa to suit their functions, reasonably priced, practical and recyclable, they are the latest must-have articles for the 21st-century kitchen.

While San Lorenzo championed silverware for cooking, Gabriele De Vecchi experimented with 'eloquent' silver while searching for new ways in which objects can communicate their function. His playful 'Slow Drink' water jugs of 2001 draw the user's attention to the process of pouring (plates 77–79). The strategically placed devices such as a miniature mill wheel in the spout or free-rolling bowls in the hollow handle ensure that each time the jugs are used, these elements move and make pleasing sounds, adding an element of play to the otherwise unremarkable task at hand. Some of

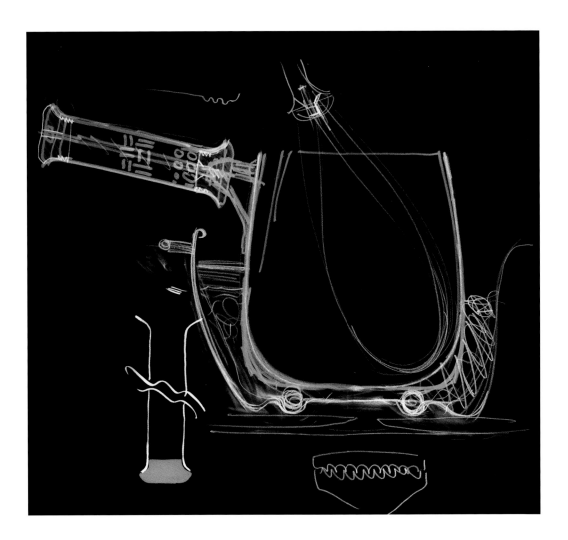

Tobia Scarpa's design drawing for a pure (999) silver saucepan and whisk (see plate 74). Note how the whisk fits snugly in the bowl.

San Lorenzo's ingenious 'Moneyware' (plates 75 & 76), which celebrate the new European currency, the Euro, work on similar principles.

Concurrently, De Vecchi was also harnessing the recent explosion of new design talent in Europe. In 2001, he invited ten designers to work on 'De Vecchi Too', a collection of contemporary articles for everyday use. All new to working with silver, the group consisted of Erwan and Ronan Bouroullec, Rodolfo Dordoni (plate 81), Tom Dixon (plate 82), Jean Marie Massaud, Patrick Norguet, Ludovica and Roberto Palomba and Patricia Urquiola. While the designers were encouraged to maintain the company's commitment to the interactive and illusory qualities of silver, the project resulted in a range of highly individual solutions, with Dordoni's place mat 'Vasarely' among the most striking outcomes. In 2002 the 'De Vecchi Too' series further expanded, with new designers enriching the inaugural range.

Just as it seemed that Italian silver was moving away from museum pedestals and into the domestic setting, 'high style' returned to the silver arena. Keen to explore domestic silver's future territories once again, in January 2002 Alessi initiated part two of its 'Tea & Coffee Piazza' series. This time, Alberto Alessi and Alessandro Mendini invited 22 internationally acclaimed architects whose work they considered 'fundamental to the debate on contemporary design'.[41] Encompassing both celebrity names and representatives of the younger generation, the group comprised Vito Acconci (USA), Will Alsop (GB), Wiel Arets (Netherlands), Shigeru Ban (Japan), Gary Chang (Hong Kong), David Chipperfield (UK), Denton Corker Marshall (Australia), Dezsö Ekler (Hungary),

Massimiliano Fuksas and Doriana Mandrelli (Italy), Future Systems (GB), Zaha Hadid (UK), Toyo Ito (Japan), Tom Kovac (Australia), Greg Lynn (USA), Morphosis (USA), M.V.R.D.V. (Netherlands), Juan Navarro Baldeweg (Spain), Jean Nouvel (France), Dominique Perrault (France), Kazuyo Sejima and Ryue Nishizawa (Japan) and Ben van Berkel and Caroline Bos (Netherlands). Alessandro Mendini completed the mighty team.

Previewed at the 8th Biennale of Architecture in Venice under the title 'City of Towers', the project revealed an astonishing variety of innovative solutions (plates 83–89). Although the majority of sets were eventually produced in sterling silver, the collection comprises sets in titanium, stainless steel, heat-resistant glass and ceramic, and also silver vessels 'enriched' with elements made of glass, thermoplastic resin, ceramic, wood and titanium. Selected silver designs may also be released in stainless steel. It is evident that the new digital tools in design have encouraged more complex, irregular forms, often conceived as singular configurations that break up like puzzles to reveal their hidden contents. Strongly architectonic or sculptural, stacked up in tall towers or nestled within voluptuous organic formations, these designs entice with their fabulous forms while, it seems, remaining perfectly functional. As if to counterbalance the more expressive and futuristic proposals, some sets are more contemplative. David Chipperfield's set, for example, includes delicate ceramic pieces which remind us of the ancient origins of tea sets and of tea drinking as a ritual (plate 87).

A mood of enchantment with the East, relating to the designer's long-standing interest in Eastern philosophies, also permeated the recent exhibition of 20 monumental silver vases and centrepieces designed by Ettore Sottsass Jr (plates 90–92). Majestic in their scale and geometric simplicity, they were made to hold a single flower or a few pieces of fruit 'as is the practice in Oriental cultures'.[42] These splendid vessels created by Rossi & Arcandi are a tribute from Sottsass, a key figure in 20th-century design, to silver as a contemporary material.

Conclusion

During the last three decades, silverware made in Italy in the modern idiom has dazzled both local and international consumers with a range of designs more varied, refined and influential than those of any other country. An ancient craft given a new life by some of the most creative architects, designers and silversmiths, Italian silver has entered the new millennium with confidence. Whether intended for the table, for use in the kitchen or destined for museums, as long as its forms excite and inspire, the lustrous metal will continue its journey into the future, as magical as ever.

Notes

1 About half was used for making jewellery. Other major producers were Germany (300 metric tonnes), the USA (250 metric tonnes) and Great Britain (90 metric tonnes). Silver articles made in Italy are usually marked with a five-point star, maker's registration number and initials of province and an oval containing silver standards: 800, 925 or 999, in addition to the maker's mark and sometimes designer's marks and date letters. Information provided by Federargentieri (Italian Federation of Silversmiths).

2 John K D Cooper, 'Silver', in *The dictionary of art*, Macmillan, London, 1996, vol 28, p 737.

3 K Painter, 'The ancient world', in C Blair, *The history of silver*, Macdonald Orbis, London, 1987, p 9.

4 The Romans called silver *Argentum* and 'Ag' remains its chemical symbol today.

5 A De Giovanni, 'Modernism lost', in T F Giacobone (ed), *Italian silverware of the 20th century: from decorative arts to design*, Electa, Milan, 1993, p 36.

6 The Monza Biennales were supported by the School of Decorative Arts in Monza, which played an important role in the revival of the decorative arts in the late 1920s and 1930s.

7 In 1930 the Monza Biennales moved to Milan, and in 1933 they became the Triennales di Milano or 'International exhibitions of modern decorative and industrial arts and architecture'. The 7th Milan Triennale of 1940 displayed only Italian products.

8 G C Argan, 'Ideological development in the thought and imagery of Italian design', in E Ambasz (ed), *Italy: the new domestic landscape*, MoMA, New York, 1972, p 363.

9 In 1947 the Communist and Socialist parties were expelled from the Combined Government which patronised anti-fascist rationalism. Conforming to the prevailing tastes of the middle classes, the Democrats preferred 'artistic' modernism in the decorative arts.

10 J Haycraft, *Italian labyrinth: Italy in the 1980s*, Secker & Warburg, London, 1985, p 103.

11 See P Sparke, *Design in Italy, 1870 to the present*, Abbeville Press, New York, 1988.

12 Designed in 1949, the 'Fasoletto' vase achieved great popularity in the 1950s.

13 Sponsored by La Rinascente, a prestigious chain of department stores, the Compasso d'Oro awards commenced in 1954.

14 Based in Bregano (Como), Lino Sabattini still continues to design and make his distinctive objects.

15 G Hughes, *Modern silver throughout the world 1880-1967*, Crown Publishers, New York, 1967, p 67.

16 Such as the Goldsmiths' Company in London.

17 Interview with Gabriele De Vecchi, January 2003.

18 Pioneered by Marcel Duchamp, Naum Gabo and Alexander Calder, kinetic art is concerned with sculptural works that include motion as a significant component.

19 Interview with Gabriele De Vecchi, January 2003.

20 Interview with Gabriele De Vecchi, January 2003.

21 E Turner, 'The silversmith's studio San Lorenzo', in *The work of the silversmith's studio San Lorenzo, Milano, 1970–1995* exhibition catalogue, Electa, Milan, 1995, p 15.

22 *The work of the silversmith's studio San Lorenzo, Milano, 1970–1995*, an exhibition at the Victoria and Albert Museum, London, 1995–96.

23 Although trained as architects, the Vignellis, who since the mid 1960s have been based in New York, have mostly worked as industrial and graphic designers.

24 Interview with Ciro Cacchione, January 2003.

25 E Turner, 'The silversmith's studio San Lorenzo', in *The work of the silversmith's studio San Lorenzo, Milano, 1970–1995*, Electa, Milan, 1995, p 19.

26 See for example F Rhelms, 'Les Italiens manient l'or et l'argent avec prudence', *Le Figaro*, 13 January 1971.

27 P Balmas, 'Interview with Cleto Munari' in A B Oliva, *La figura delle cose: Cleto Munari in Castel Sant' Angelo*, Electa, Naples, 1999, p 32.

28 P Balmas, p 36.

29 Harder than gold but softer than copper, silver is usually combined with copper to make a harder alloy for silverware and jewellery. The two common standards are 925 (sterling silver) and 800. Sterling silver contains 92.5% silver and 7.5% copper.

30 B Radice, *Memphis*, Thames & Hudson, New York, 1995, p 67.

31 C Jencks, 'New international style e altare etichette', *Domus*, no 623, December 1981, p 44.

32 P Glanville, *Silver*, Victoria and Albert Museum, London, 1996, p 78.

33 R. Meier, 'Alberto Alessi's factory journal, November 1993', quoted in *Alessi, the design factory*, Academy Editions, London, 1994, p 39.

34 In 1986 Mateo Thun used the same idea for his 'walking coffeepots' design, made in silver-plated brass for the German manufacturer WMF.

35 From 1992, Munari's 'Masterpieces' have been crafted in his own workshop in Vincenza and sold to collectors by Cleto Munari Associati SRL.

36 Interview with Giovanni Baule in T F Giacobone (ed), *La lingua degli specchi*, Electa, Milan, 1997, p 127.

37 E Turner, 'The silversmith's studio of San Lorenzo', in *The work of the silversmith's studio San Lorenzo, Milano*, Electa, Milan, 1995, p 19.

38 Through the St/Art collection developed by Gabriele De Vecchi between 1992 and 1997, he also collaborated with graduates from Milanese design schools, thus providing them with invaluable practical experience.

39 Interview with Giovanni Baule, in T F Giacobone (ed), *La lingua degli specchi*, Electa, Milan, 1997, p 123.

40 Interview with Cleto Munari, January 2003.

41 Stefano Casciani's interview with Alessandro Mendini, 'Next object', www.alessi.it

42 Ettore Sottsass, *20 argenti grandi*, exhibition at the Gallery Paolo Curti/Annamaria Gambuzzi & Co, Milan, 25 Sept to 10 Nov 2002.

The Plates

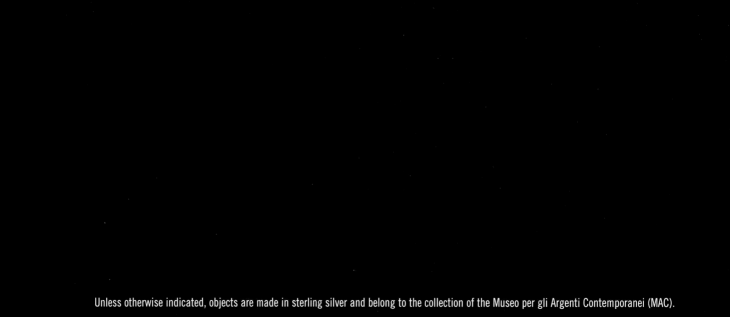

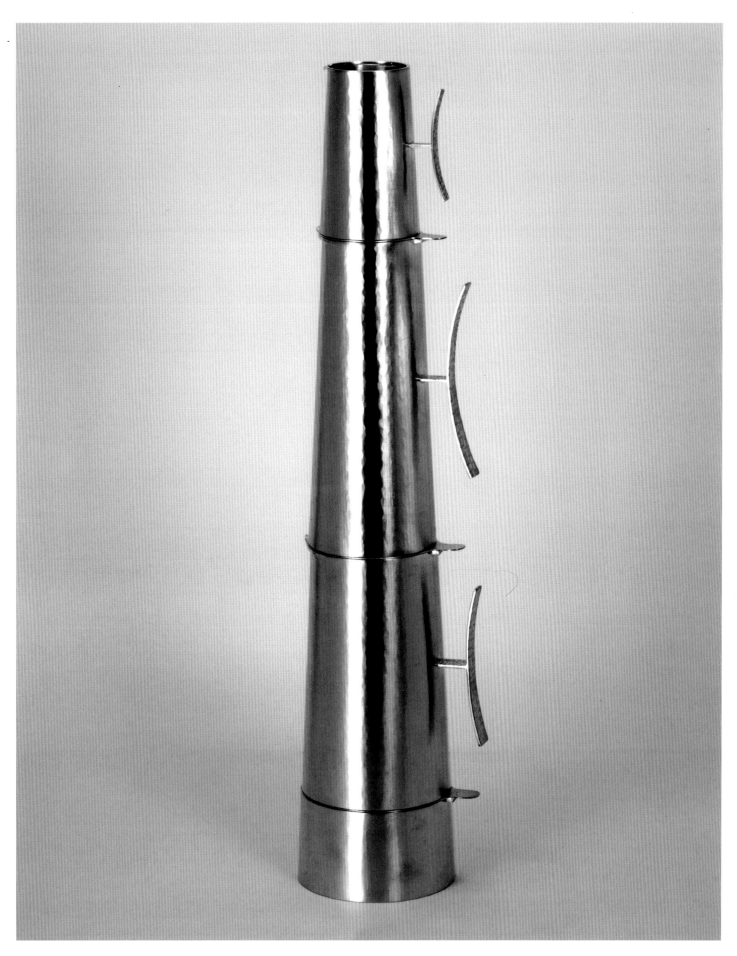

PLATE 1 Stackable tea and coffee service, 'Manhattan', designed by Olga Finzi, made by Finzi Arte in Milan in 1957. When assembled as a 'tower', the set can be used as a vase. Assembled service 51.5 cm (h).

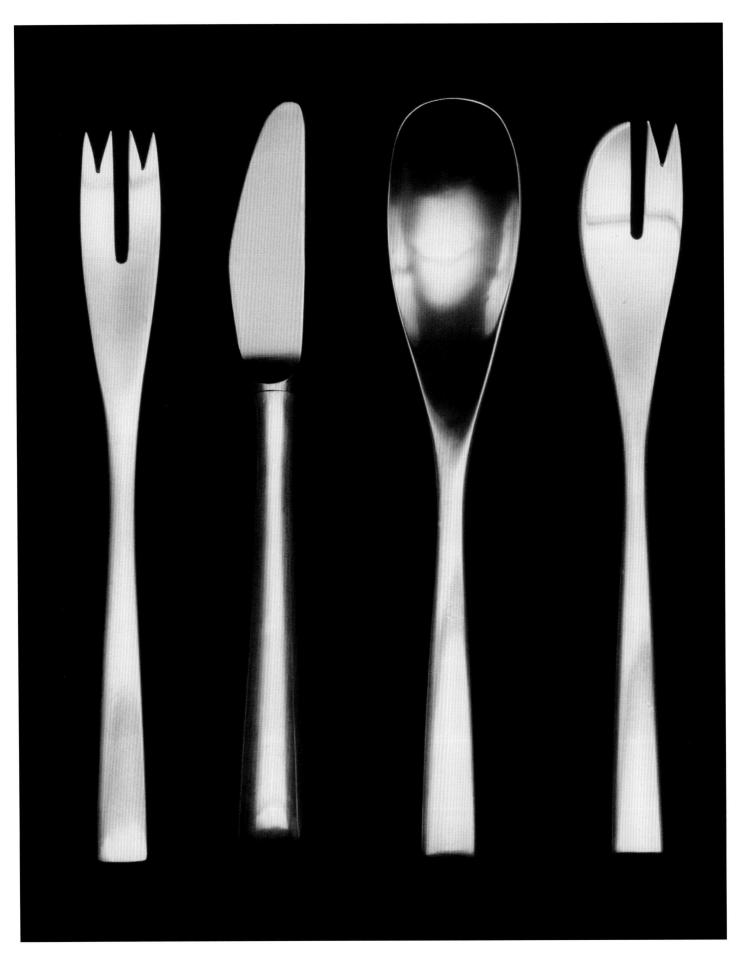

PLATE 2 Cutlery, 'Elite', designed and made by Olga Finzi Baldi in Milan between 1967 and 1969. Cutlery 20 cm (l).

Photo courtesy of Olga Finzi Baldi.

PLATE 3 Beakers, 'Elite', designed and made by Olga Finzi Baldi in Milan in the 1960s. The tallest beaker has a small bell in the hollow base.

Photo courtesy of Olga Finzi Baldi.

PLATE 4 Desk lamp, 'New Form' collection, designed by Corinna Morandi and Gabriele De Vecchi in 1971, made by De Vecchi in Milan. Lamp 28 cm (h).

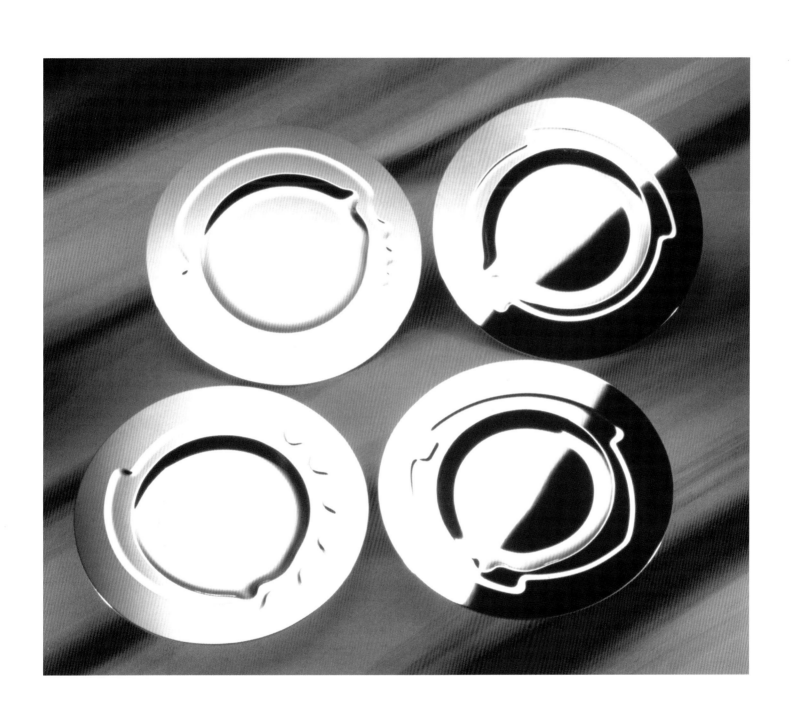

PLATE 5 Plates, 'Minimal' collection, designed by Corinna Morandi and Gabriele De Vecchi in 1971, made by De Vecchi in Milan.

Photo courtesy of the Museo per gli Argenti Contemporanei (MAC).

PLATE 6 Jug, 'H$_2$O', 'Minimal' collection, designed by Gabriele De Vecchi in 1975 and made by De Vecchi in Milan. Jug 20 cm (w).

Photo by Leo Torri, courtesy of De Vecchi.

PLATE 7 Two vases, 'Phoemina' and 'Diana', 'Minimal' collection, designed by Gabriele De Vecchi in 1978 and made by De Vecchi in Milan. 'Phoemina' vase 25 cm (h).

Photo courtesy of De Vecchi.

PLATE 8 Tableware designed by Antonio Piva for San Lorenzo, Milan, 1970–72.

Photo courtesy of San Lorenzo.

PLATE 9 Tea and coffee service designed by Franco Albini and Franca Helg for San Lorenzo, Milan, 1971. Coffeepot 20 cm (h). This is one of the first architect-designed silver tea and coffee sets made in the 1970s.

Photo courtesy of San Lorenzo.

PLATE 10 Bowls, 'Pannocchia' (Corncob), decorated in the repoussé (hammering) technique, designed by Franco Albini and Franca Helg for San Lorenzo, Milan, 1971. Bowls 6 cm to 54 cm (diam).

PLATE 11 Bar set, comprising champagne and ice buckets, jugs, a cocktail shaker and jiggers, designed by Massimo and Lella Vignelli for San Lorenzo, Milan, 1971. Champagne bucket 25 cm (h).

Photo courtesy of San Lorenzo.

PLATE 12 Covered boxes, silver and copper, designed by Afra and Tobia Scarpa for San Lorenzo, Milan, 1972. Boxes 3.5 cm and 6.5 cm (h). Collection: San Lorenzo.

Photo courtesy of San Lorenzo.

PLATE 13 Set of polygonal vases, designed by Afra and Tobia Scarpa for San Lorenzo, Milan, 1971. Tallest vase 18 cm (h).

Photo courtesy of San Lorenzo.

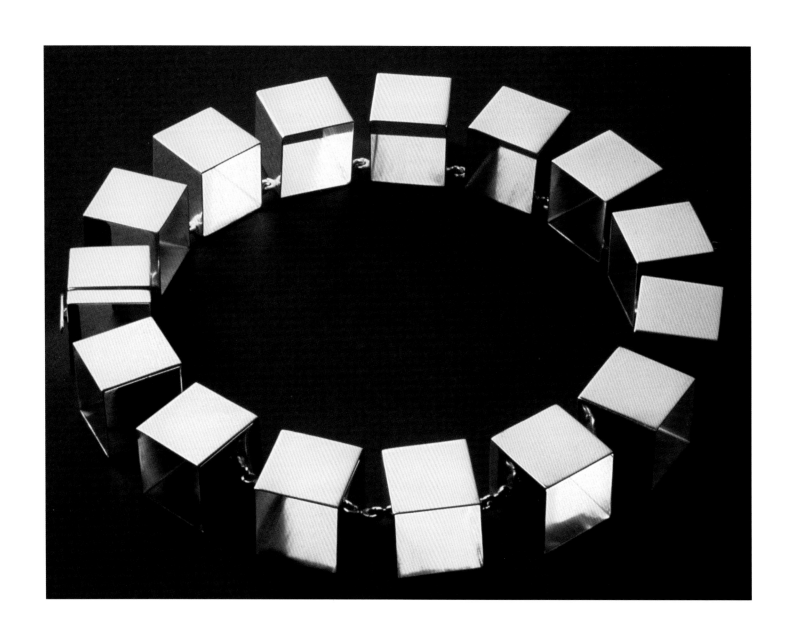

PLATE 14 Necklace designed by Lella and Massimo Vignelli for San Lorenzo, Milan, 1971. Necklace 12 cm (diam). Besides silverware, San Lorenzo has also produced silver jewellery. The 2003 autumn collection was designed by twelve women designers.

Photo courtesy of San Lorenzo.

PLATE 15 Cutlery and jug with silver-gilt interior designed by Carlo Scarpa (1906–78) for Cleto Munari, made by Rossi & Arcandi, Vicenza, 1977–78.

Photo courtesy of the Museo per gli Argenti Contemporanei (MAC) and Cleto Munari Design Associati.

PLATE 16 Tea and coffee set in silver and rosewood designed by Ettore Sottsass Jr for Cleto Munari, made by Rossi & Arcandi, Vicenza, 1971–81.

Photo courtesy of the Museo per gli Argenti Contemporanei (MAC) and Cleto Munari Design Associati.

PLATE 17 Covered jug in silver and plastics designed by Michele De Lucchi for Cleto Munari, made by Rossi & Arcandi, Vicenza, 1979–80 (see also p 19).

Photo courtesy of the Museo per gli Argenti Contemporanei (MAC) and Cleto Munari Design Associati.

PLATE 18 Vase, 'Alaska', designed by Ettore Sottsass Jr for Memphis, made by Rossi & Arcandi, Vicenza, 1982. Vase 30 cm (h).

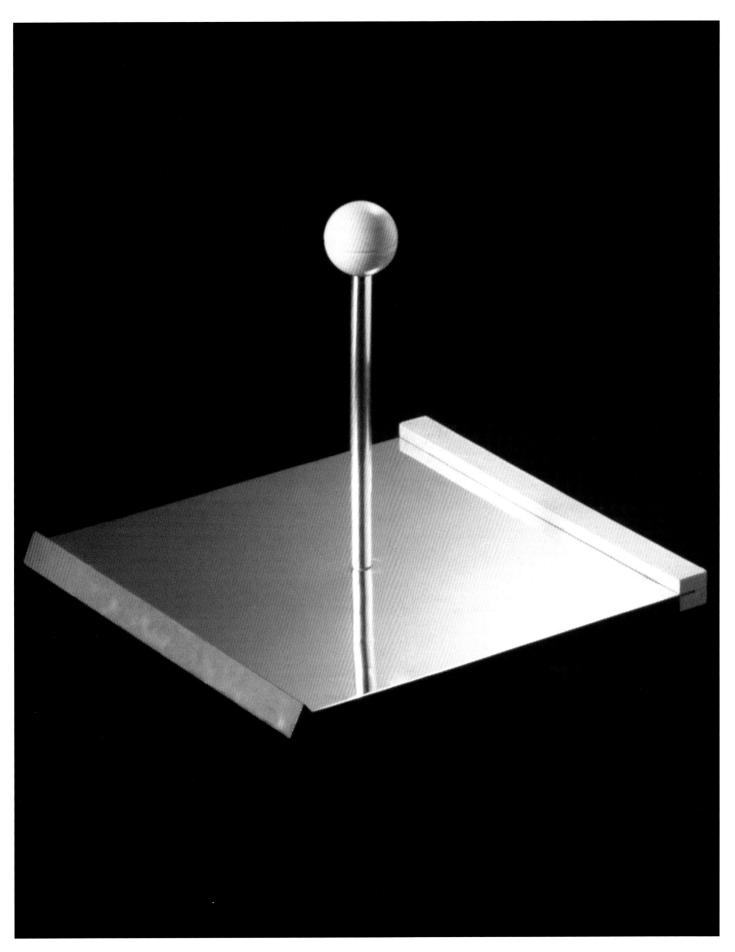

PLATE 19 Tray, 'Antarctic', in silver and wood, designed by Daniela Puppa for Memphis, made by Rossi & Arcandi, Vicenza, 1982. Tray 23 cm (h).

PLATE 20 Sauceboat, 'Labrador', in silver and glass, designed by Andrea Branzi for Memphis, made by Rossi & Arcandi, Vicenza, 1982. Sauceboat 40 cm (h).

Photo courtesy of Memphis SRL, Milan.

PLATE 21 Teapot, 'Anchorage', in silver, metal and wood, designed by Peter Shire for Memphis, made by Rossi & Arcandi, Vicenza, 1982. Teapot 40 cm (h).

Photo courtesy of Memphis SRL, Milan.

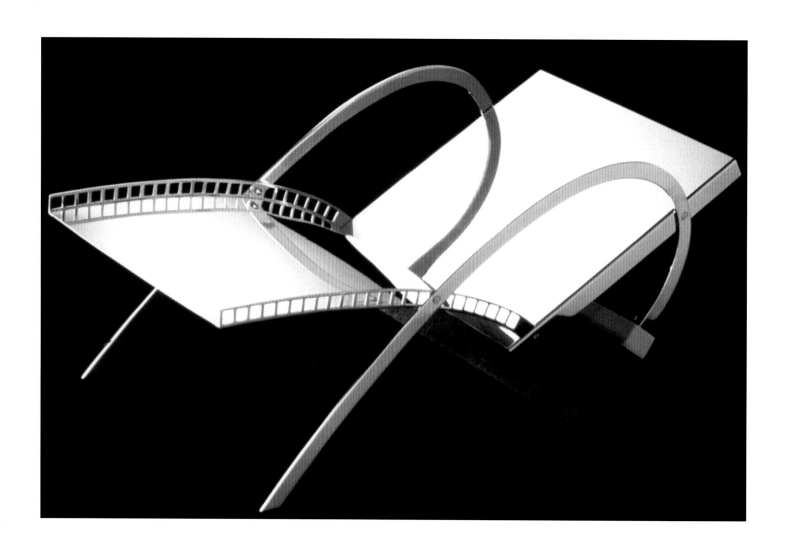

PLATE 22 Fruit bowl, 'Bering', in silver and marble, designed by Matteo Thun for Memphis, made by Rossi & Arcandi, Vicenza, 1982. Fruit bowl 20 cm (h).

Photo courtesy Memphis SRL, Milan.

PLATE 23 Fruit stand, 'Murmansk', designed by Ettore Sottsass Jr for Memphis about 1982, made in electroplated silver by Rossi & Arcandi, Vicenza, about 1987 (see also p 20). Stand 27.5 cm (h). Collection: Powerhouse Museum, Sydney. 86/1018.

Photo by Sue Stafford, Powerhouse Museum

PLATE 24 'Tea & Coffee Piazza', made in silver, iron, brass, copper and quartz, designed by Aldo Rossi for Alessi in 1983. Made in 1997, number 42 in a limited edition of 99. Case 64 cm (h). The designs for the teapot and coffeepot allude to Rossi's 'Teatro del mondo', a floating theatre of wood and steel built for the 1980 Venice Biennale. The design for the case was inspired by his architectural model 'Il teatrino scientifico' of 1978 (see p 24). Collection: Powerhouse Museum, the Alitalia Collection, 1997. 97/210

Photo by Sue Stafford, Powerhouse Museum

PLATE 25 'Tea & Coffee Piazza', in silver, blue-lacquered aluminium, black bakelite, imitation ivory and glass (tray), designed by Michael Graves in 1983 and made by Alessi. Coffepot 24.5 cm (h). Collection: Museo Alessi.

Photo by Aldo Ballo, courtesy of Alessi.

PLATE 26 'Tea & Coffee Piazza', designed by Paolo Portoghesi in 1983 and made by Alessi. Coffeepot and teapot 16.5 cm (h). Collection: Museo Alessi.

Photo by Aldo Ballo, courtesy of Alessi.

PLATE 27 'Tea & Coffee Piazza', in silver and imitation ivory, designed by Richard Meier in 1983 and made by Alessi. Coffeepot 22.5 cm (h). Collection: Museo Alessi.

Photo by Aldo Ballo, courtesy of Alessi.

PLATE 28 'Tea & Coffee Piazza', designed by Hans Hollein in 1983 and made by Alessi. The tray, resembling the deck of an aircraft carrier, is made in silver electroplated brass. Handles and feet in methacrylate. Teapot 18 cm (h). Collection: Museo Alessi.

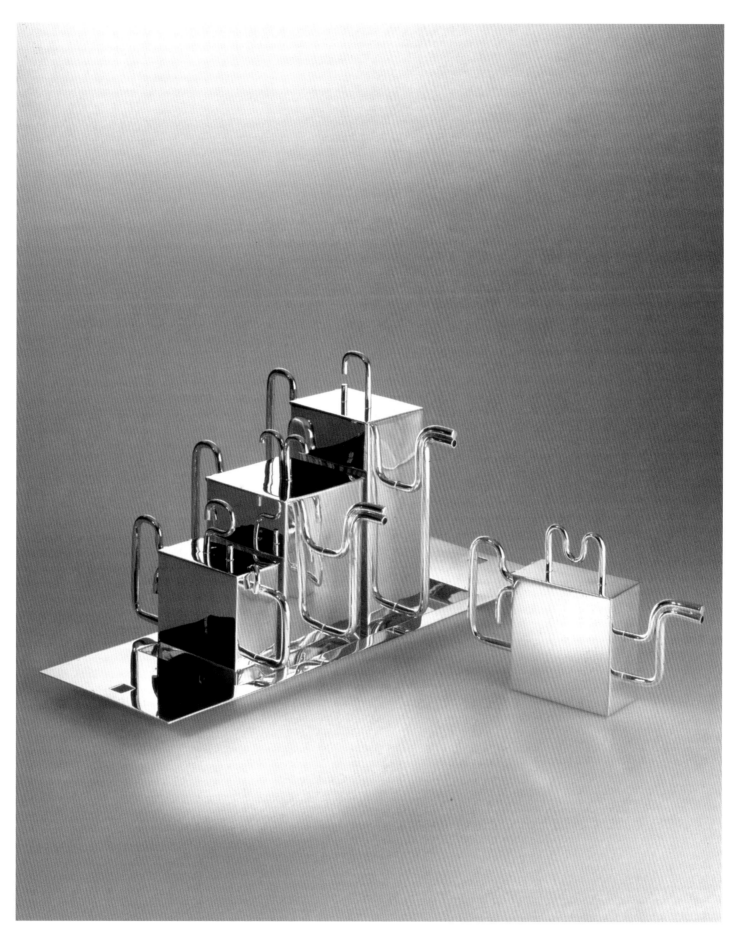

PLATE 29 'Tea & Coffee Piazza', designed by Kazumasa Yamashita in 1983 and made by Alessi. Coffeepot 22.5 cm (h). Collection: Museo Alessi.

Photo by Aldo Ballo, courtesy of Alessi.

PLATE 30 'Tea & Coffee Piazza', designed by Charles Jencks in 1983 and made by Alessi. Coffeepot 22 cm (h). Collection: Museo Alessi.

Photo by Aldo Ballo, courtesy of Alessi.

PLATE 31 'Tea & Coffee Piazza', silver, ebony and gilt, designed by Robert Venturi for Alessi in 1983. Coffeepot 21.5 cm (h). Consistent with the postmodern architect's proclamation that 'less is a bore', a paraphrase of Ludwig Mies van der Rohe's modernist credo 'less is more', this set is richly decorated with mechanically engraved floral motifs inlaid with gold. The tray is made in gold-plated stainless steel. The handles, spouts and knobs are cast in the lost wax technique (see also p 23). Collection: Museo Alessi.

Photo by Aldo Ballo, courtesy of Alessi.

PLATE 32 'Tea & Coffee Piazza', designed by Stanley Tigerman in 1983 and made by Alessi. Coffeepot 19.5 cm (h). Collection: Museo Alessi.

Photo by Aldo Ballo, courtesy of Alessi.

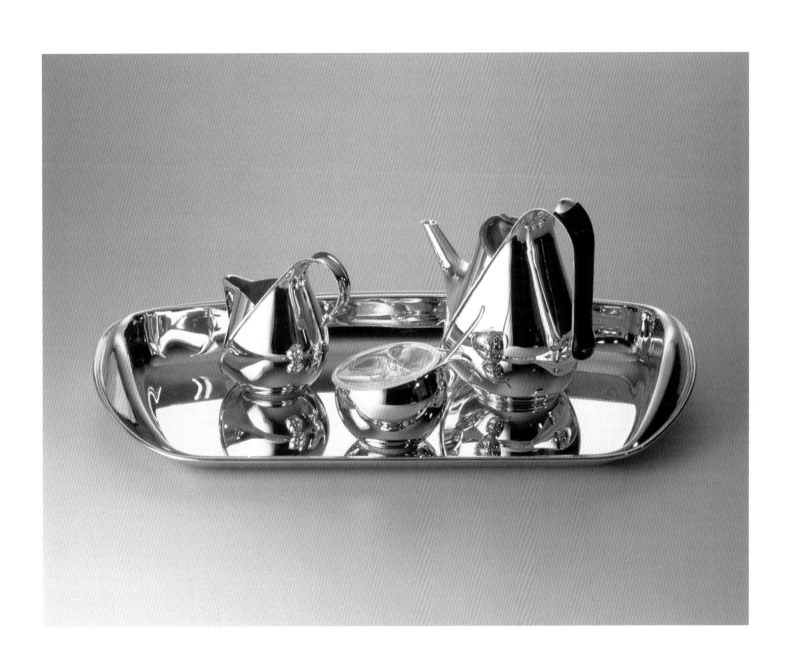

PLATE 33 Coffee set from the 'Tea & Coffee Piazza' series, in silver and ebony, designed by Oscar Tusquets in 1983 and made by Alessi. Coffeepot 19 cm (h). The bodies of the coffeepot and creamer are made from two welded shells with riveting along the seam. Collection: Museo Alessi.

Photo by Aldo Ballo, courtesy of Alessi.

PLATE 34 'Tea and Coffee Piazza', designed by Alessandro Mendini for Alessi in 1983. Coffeepot 24 cm (h) (see also p 22). Collection: Museo Alessi.

Photo by Aldo Ballo, courtesy of Alessi.

PLATE 35 Teapot from the 'Pinguino' (Penguin) tea set in silver and wood designed by Matteo Thun for Cleto Munari, made by Rossi & Arcandi, Vicenza, in 1983.

Photo courtesy of Cleto Munari Design Associati.

PLATE 36 Candlesticks designed by Alessandro Mendini for Cleto Munari, made by Rossi & Arcandi, Vicenza, in 1989.

Photo courtesy of the Museo per gli Argenti Contemporanei (MAC) and Cleto Munari Design Associati.

PLATE 37 Pair of vases designed by Angelo Mangiarotti for Cleto Munari, made by Rossi & Arcandi, Vicenza, in 1981.

Photo courtesy of the Museo per gli Argenti Contemporanei (MAC) and Cleto Munari Design Associati.

PLATE 38 Champagne and ice buckets designed by Giotto Stoppino for Cleto Munari, made by Rossi & Arcandi, Vicenza, in 1983.

PLATE 39 Pair of jugs designed by Mario Botta for Cleto Munari, made by Rossi & Arcandi, Vicenza, in 1987.

Photo courtesy of Cleto Munari Design Associati.

PLATE 40 Jug, 'Anselmo', 'Speriment' series, in silver with plastic industrial handle, designed by Gabriele De Vecchi in 1982, made by De Vecchi in Milan. Jug 18 cm (w).

Photo courtesy of the Museo per gli Argenti Contemporanei (MAC).

PLATE 41 Teapot, 'Emisfera', 'Speriment' series, designed by Gabriele De Vecchi in 1985, made by De Vecchi in Milan. Teapot 17 cm (h).

Photo courtesy of de Vecchi.

PLATE 42 Candlestick, 'Speriment' series, designed by Gabriele De Vecchi in 1985, made by De Vecchi in Milan.

Photo courtesy of De Vecchi.

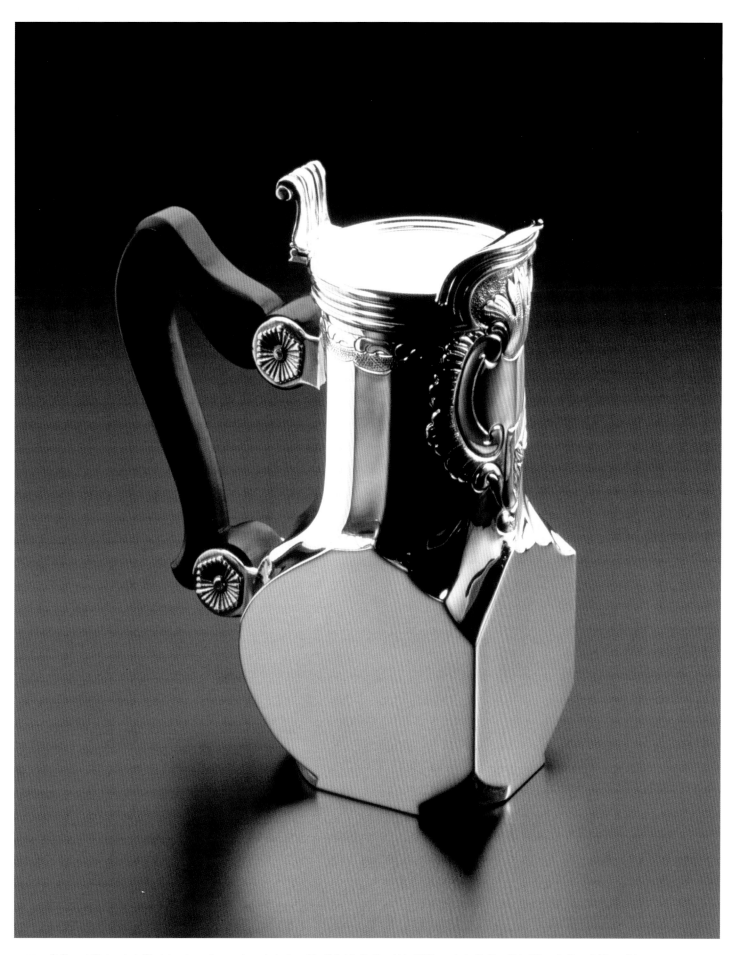

PLATE 43 Coffeepot 'Torincubo', 'Storia' series, silver and wood, designed by Gabriele De Vecchi in 1985, made by De Vecchi in Milan. Coffeepot 18 cm (h).

Photo courtesy of De Vecchi.

PLATE 44 Coffeepot, 'Ivizo', silver and wood, 'Storia' series, designed by Gabriele De Vecchi for 'A sparkling party' competition in Antwerp in 1993 and made by De Vecchi in Milan. Coffeepot 19 cm (h).

PLATE 45 Vase, 'Quadro', 'Minimal' series, designed by Gabriele De Vecchi in 1986, made by De Vecchi in Milan. Vase 22 cm (h).

Photo by Leo Torri, courtesy of De Vecchi.

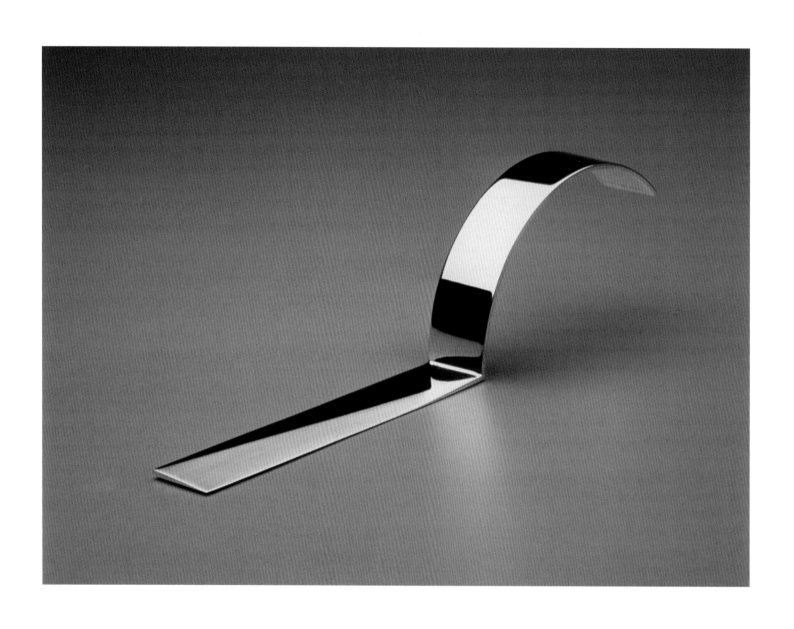

PLATE 46 Letter opener, 'Excalibur', designed by Carla Venosta in 1989 and made by De Vecchi in Milan. Selected for the 15th Compasso d'Oro. Opener 24 cm (l).

Photo courtesy of the Museo per gli Argenti Contemporanei (MAC).

PLATE 47 Covered boxes, 'Guillochis' (Guilloche), designed by Maria Luisa Belgiojoso for San Lorenzo, Milan, 1986. Tallest box 5.1 cm (h). The decoration on the surface is made using an 18th century technique of bright-cut engraving. Collection: San Lorenzo

PLATE 48 Wine and milk jugs and sugar bowls, 'Moretta', with gilt interior. Designed by Afra and Tobia Scarpa, made by San Lorenzo in 1990. Tallest jug 15 cm (h). Moretta is the name of a character from the Venetian carnivale. The forms of these vessels resemble a Moretta mask turned upside down. The innovative textured surface is achieved with the aid of five purpose-designed punches.

Photo courtesy of San Lorenzo.

PLATE 49 Tea and coffee set in silver and bakelite designed by Laura Handler (USA) in 1985, made by Pomellato in Venice in 1990.

Photo courtesy of Pomellato.

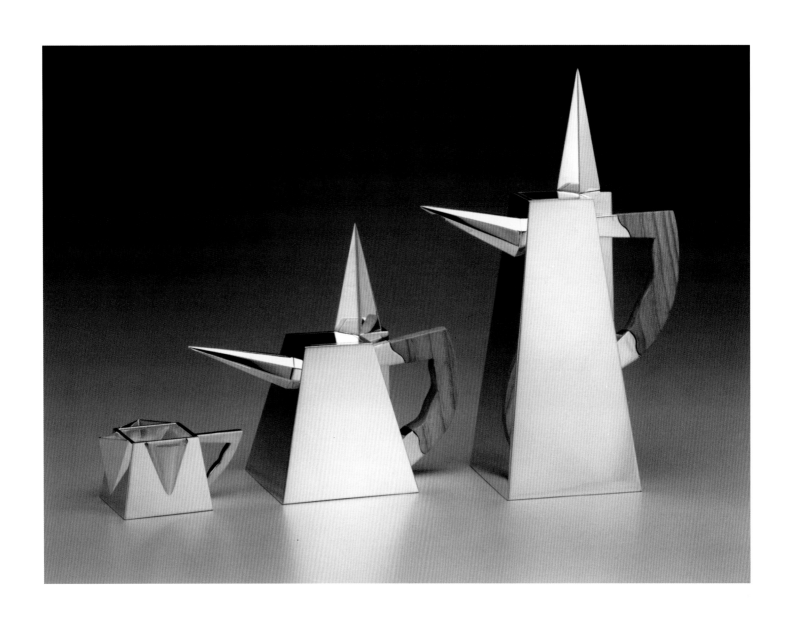

PLATE 50 Tea and coffee set, 'Pinochieide' (Pinnochio), in silver and wood, designed by Lapo Binazzi, made by Pampaloni in Florence in 1987.

PLATE 51 Ice bucket designed by Claudio Salocchi, made by Gemma Gioielli in Verona in 1992.

PLATE 52 Candlesticks, 'Segnico', designed by Claudio Salocchi, made by Gemma Gioielli in Verona in 1989.

PLATE 53 Serving tables, 'I segni' (The signs), designed by Claudio Salocchi, made by Gemma Gioielli in Verona in 1992.

Photo courtesy of the Museo per gli Argenti Contemporanei (MAC).

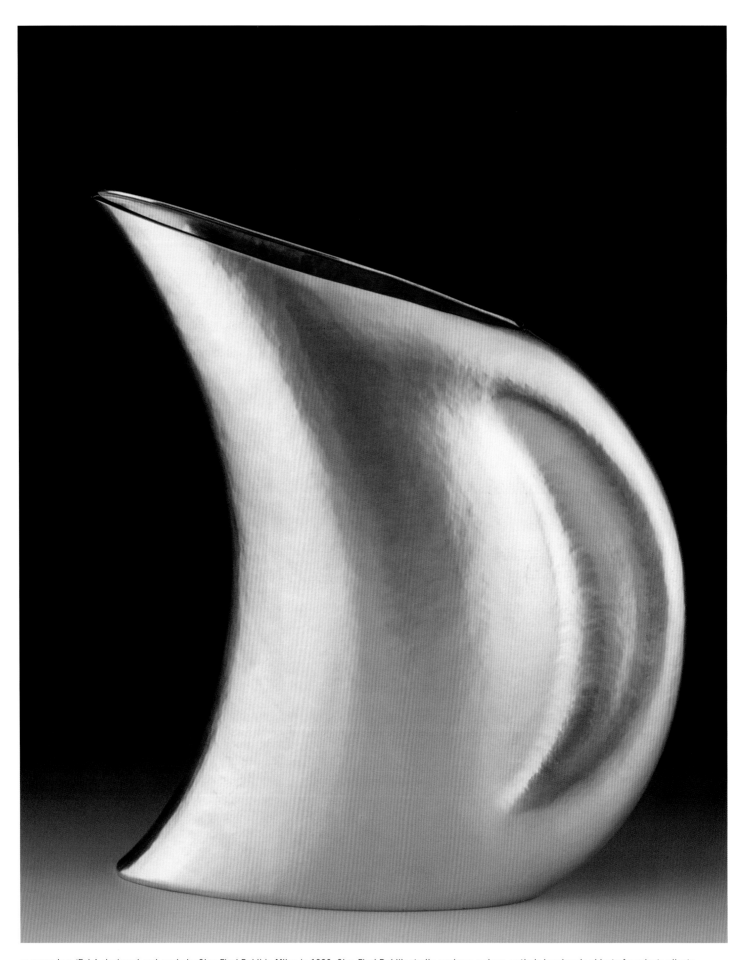

PLATE 54 Jug, 'Eolo', designed and made by Olga Finzi Baldi in Milan in 1986. Olga Finzi Baldi's studio produces unique, entirely handmade objects for private clients.

PLATE 55 Jug, 'Le diable en tête' (The devil in the head), designed by William Sawaya in 1992 and made by Sawaya and Moroni in Milan. Jug 26 cm (h). Collection: Sawaya and Moroni Spa.

Photo courtesy of Sawaya and Moroni Spa.

PLATE 56 Bread dish, 'Graph', and centrepiece, 'Paragraph', designed by Massimo Zucchi in 1990 and made by Sawaya and Moroni in Milan. Dish 11 cm (diam), centrepiece 30 cm (diam). Collection: Sawaya and Moroni Spa.

Photo courtesy of Sawaya and Moroni Spa.

PLATE 57 Champagne bucket for three bottles designed by Jean Nouvel in 1995 and made by Sawaya and Moroni in Milan in 1996. Bucket 25 cm (h). Collection: Sawaya and Moroni Spa.

Photo courtesy of Sawaya and Moroni Spa.

PLATE 58 Tea and coffee set designed by Zaha Hadid in 1995 and made by Sawaya and Moroni in Milan in 1997. This is number 3 in a limited edition of 40. Set assembled 27 cm (h). Collection: Powerhouse Museum, Sydney. 98/42/1.

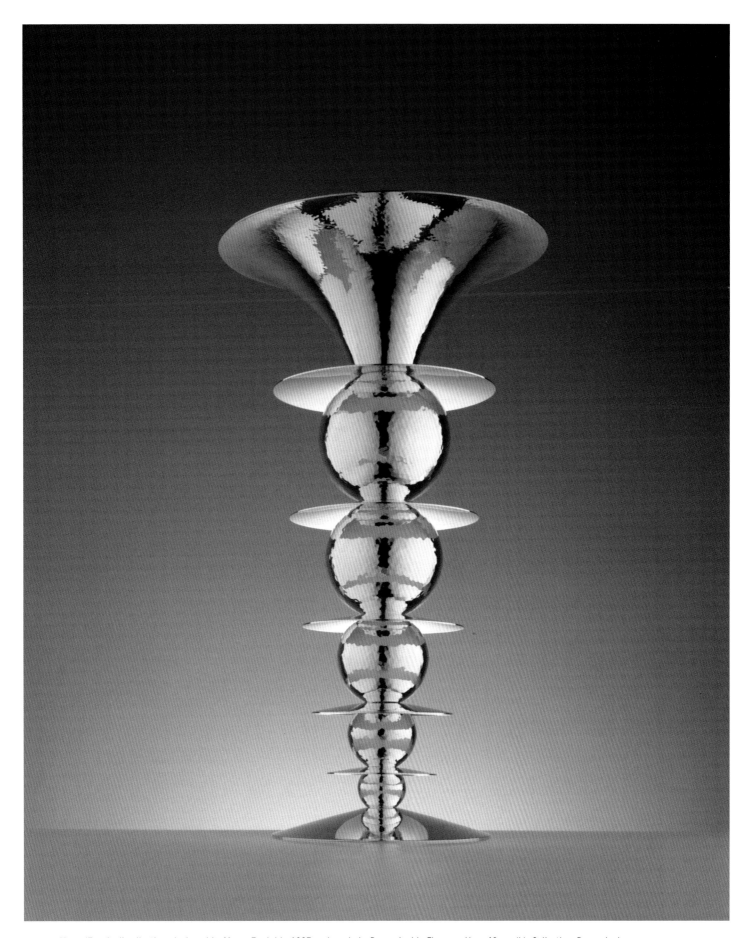

PLATE 59 Vase, 'Evasioni' collection, designed by Marco Zanini in 1997 and made by Pampaloni in Florence. Vase 42 cm (h). Collection: Pampaloni.

Photo courtesy of Gianfranco Pampaloni.

PLATE 60 Candlestick, 'Evoluzioni' collection, designed by Ettore Sottsass Jr in 1997 and made by Pampaloni in Florence. Candlestick 36 cm (h).
Collection: Pampaloni.

Photo courtesy of Gianfranco Pampaloni.

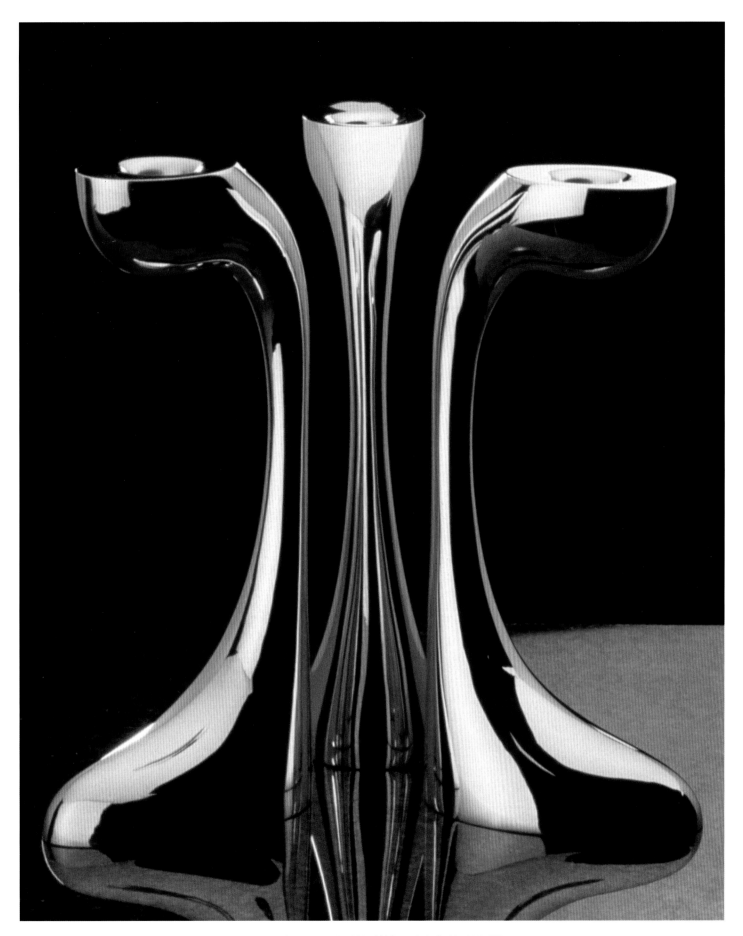

PLATE 61 Candlesticks, 'Petalo', 'Minimal' collection designed by Gabriele De Vecchi in 1990, made by De Vecchi in Milan.

Photo courtesy of De Vecchi.

PLATE 62 Jug, 'Klute', designed by Ugo La Pietra in 1991, made by De Vecchi in Milan. Jug 19.5 cm (h).

Photo courtesy of De Vecchi.

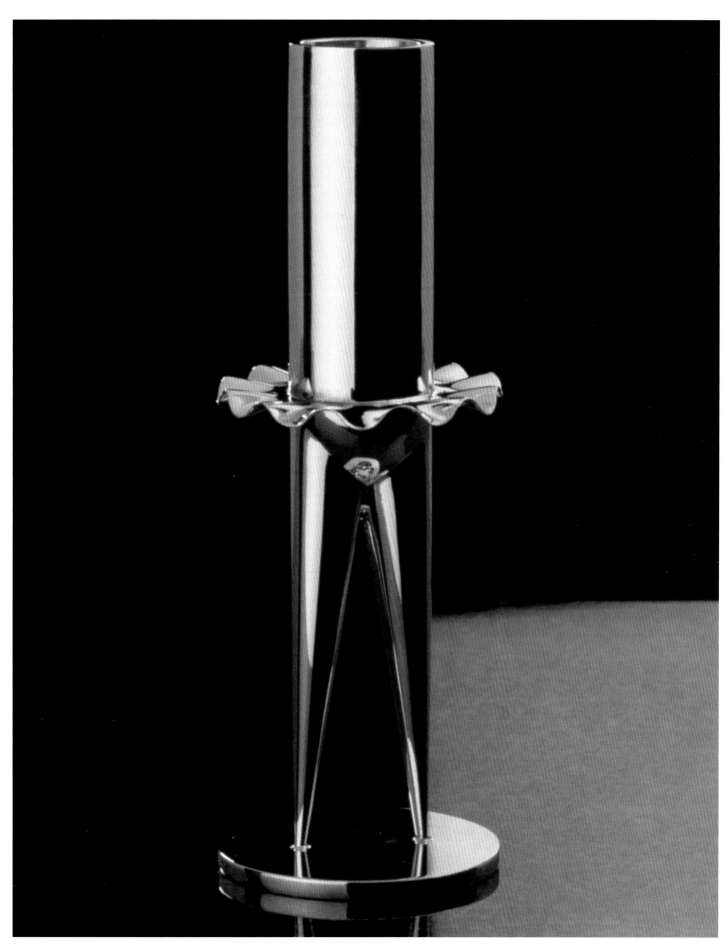

PLATE 63 Candlestick, 'Ballerina', designed by Ugo La Pietra in 1991, made by De Vecchi in Milan. Candlestick 16.5 cm (h).

Photo courtesy of De Vecchi.

PLATE 64 Covered bon-bon bowl designed by Sergio Asti in 1993, made by De Vecchi in Milan. Covered bowl 18 cm (h).

Photo courtesy of De Vecchi.

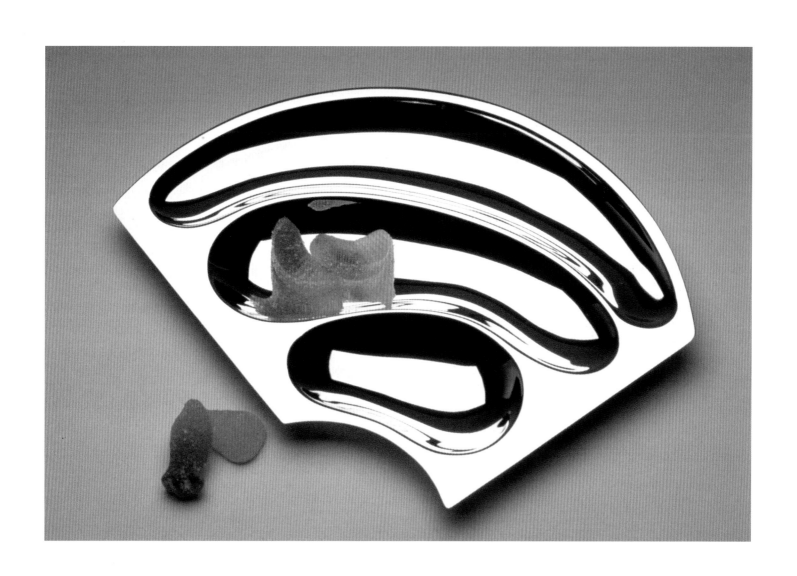

PLATE 65 Serving tray, 'Margherita', designed by Sergio Asti in 1998, made by De Vecchi in Milan. Tray 26 cm (w). Collection: De Vecchi.

Photo courtesy of De Vecchi.

PLATE 66 Fruit stand, 'Shadow of time', in silver and glass, designed by Giorgio Branca, made by Mazzucato in Milan in 1993. Stand 45 cm (h). MAC Collection '93.

Photo courtesy of the Museo per gli Argenti Contemporanei (MAC).

PLATE 67 Fruit stand designed by Sergio Asti in 1991, made by Argenteria Miracoli in Milan in 1993. Stand 15 cm (h). MAC Collection '93.

Photo courtesy of the Museo per gli Argenti Contemporanei (MAC).

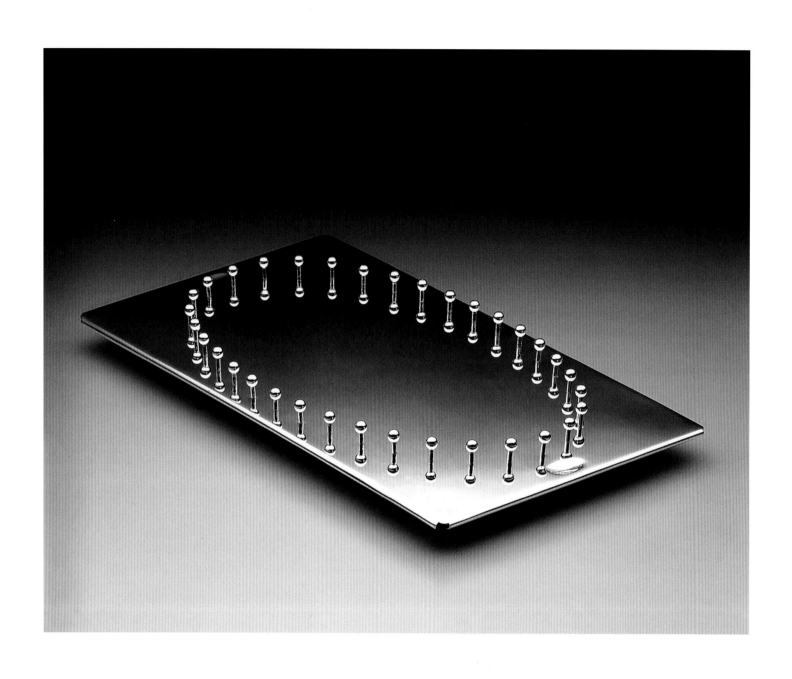

PLATE 68 Tray, 'Stonehenge', designed by Cortesi Design, made by Argenteria G Vavassori in Milan in 1993. Tray 50 cm (l) 28 cm (w). MAC Collection '93.

Photo courtesy of the Museo per gli Argenti Contemporanei (MAC).

PLATE 69 Centrepiece, 'Giasone' (Jason), designed by Claudio Brambilla, made by Argenteria M Poli in Milan in 1993. Centrepiece 27 cm (h). MAC Collection '93.

Photo courtesy of the Museo per gli Argenti Contemporanei (MAC).

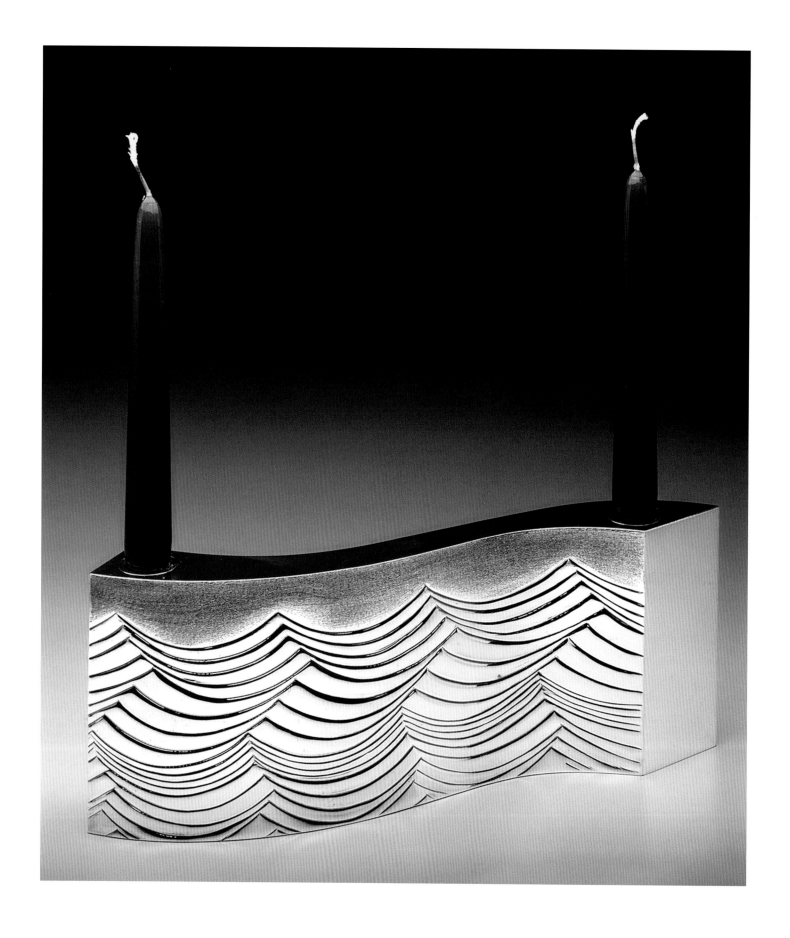

PLATE 70 Double candlestick, 'Onde' (Waves), designed by Massimo Zucchi and made by Argenteria M Vallé in Milan in 1993. Candlestick 12 cm (h). MAC Collection '93.

Photo courtesy of the Museo per gli Argenti Contemporanei (MAC) and Vallé Mario SNC.

PLATE 71 Bowls, pure (999) silver, designed by Afra and Tobia Scarpa for San Lorenzo in Milan in 1992. Largest 4.5 cm (h).

PLATE 72 Vases and bowl, pure (999) silver, designed by Afra and Tobia Scarpa for San Lorenzo in Milan in 1996. Taller vase 23 cm (h).

Photo courtesy of San Lorenzo.

PLATE 73 Candelabrum, 'Centrotavola' (Centrepiece), with adjustable branches for 15 candles. Made in pure (999) silver, bronze and iron, it utilises the reflective qualities of polished silver to the full. Designed by Afra and Tobia Scarpa for a Spanish cottage with no electricity, it was made by San Lorenzo in Milan in 1992. Candelabrum 18.5 cm (h).

Photo courtesy of San Lorenzo.

PLATE 74 Saucepan and risotto pot in pure (999) silver and titanium, part of the 'Cooking in pure silver' range designed by Afra and Tobia Scarpa in 1997–98 and made by San Lorenzo in Milan in 1999. Saucepan 21 cm (h). Design drawings in the background (see also pp 27 & 28). Collection: San Lorenzo.

Photo courtesy of San Lorenzo.

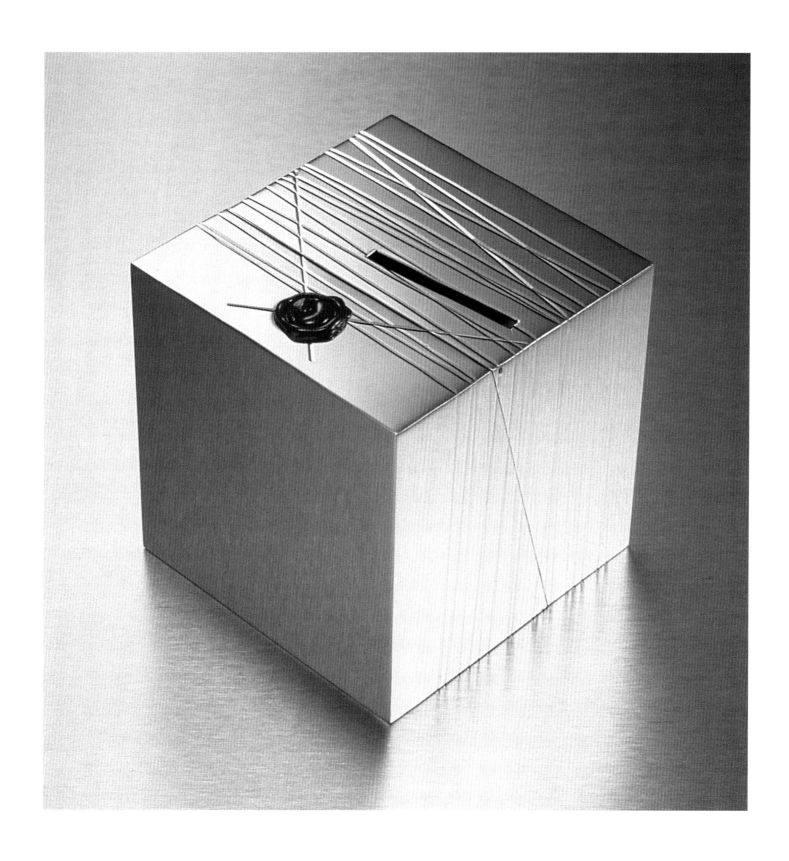

PLATE 75 Moneybox, 'SE.SA.MO' from the 'Moneyware' series, designed by Luigi Baroli for San Lorenzo in Milan in 2000. Moneybox 10 cm (h). Limited edition.
Collection: San Lorenzo.

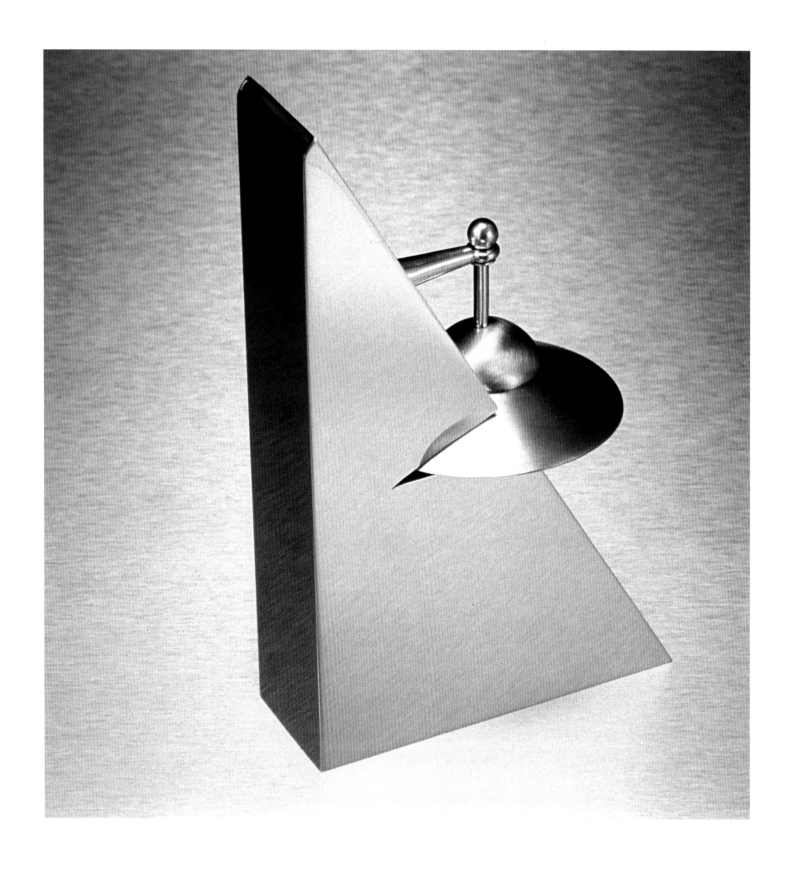

PLATE 76 Moneybox, 'Musina' (Venetian dialect for a money box) from the 'Moneyware' series, designed by Afra and Tobia Scarpa for San Lorenzo in Milan in 2000. Moneybox 18 cm (h). The design incorporates a small bell which rings each time a coin is deposited in the box. Limited edition. Collection: San Lorenzo.

Photo by Yoshie Nashikawa, courtesy of San Lorenzo.

PLATE 77 Jug, 'Moulin', from the 'Slow drink' series, designed by Gabriele De Vecchi in 2001 and made by De Vecchi in Milan. The jug has a small mill wheel in the spout. Collection: De Vecchi.

Photo by Leo Torri, courtesy of De Vecchi.

PLATE 78 Jug, 'Sound' from the 'Slow drink' series, designed by Gabriele De Vecchi in 2001 and made by De Vecchi in Milan. The jug has small balls in the handle which roll up the handle and make a sound when the jug is used. Collection: De Vecchi.

Photo by Leo Torri, courtesy of De Vecchi.

PLATE 79 Jug, 'Trebok' from the 'Slow drink' series, designed by Gabriele De Vecchi in 2001, made by De Vecchi in Milan. Collection: De Vecchi.

Photo by Leo Torri, courtesy of De Vecchi.

PLATE 80 Kettle, 'Musi', in silver and olive wood, designed by Gabriele De Vecchi in 2002, made by De Vecchi in Milan. Collection: De Vecchi.

Photos by Leo Torri, courtesy of De Vecchi.

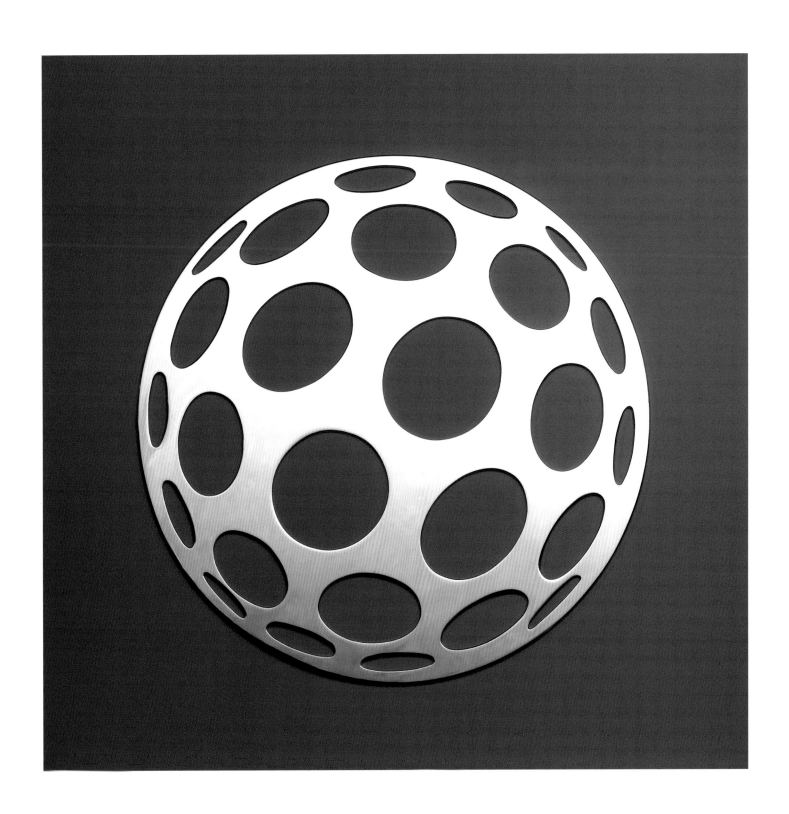

PLATE 81 Place mat, 'Vasarely', from the 'De Vecchi Too' series, designed by Rodolfo Dordoni in 2002 and made by De Vecchi in Milan. Place mat 22 cm (diam).
Collection: De Vecchi.

Photo by Leo Torri, courtesy of De Vecchi.

PLATE 82 Vase, 'Tube' from the 'De Vecchi Too' collection, designed by Tom Dixon in London in 2002 and made by De Vecchi in Milan. Vase 29 cm (h). Collection: De Vecchi.

Photo by Leo Torri, courtesy of De Vecchi.

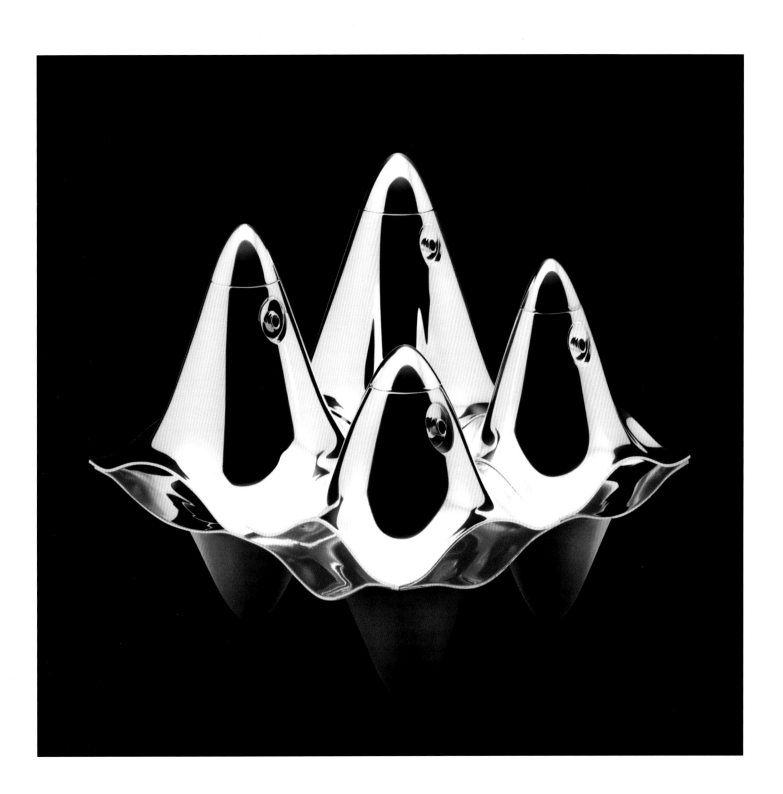

PLATE 83 Tea and coffee set from the 'Tea & Coffee Towers' series designed by Tom Kovac in Melbourne, Australia, in 2003 for Alessi. The teapot, coffeepot, sugar bowl, milk jug and tray assemble to form a single unit and are dismantled for use. The tray is the binding element of the design. Designed digitally, the shapes of individual elements are defined by a parametrically controlled geometry, the 'DNA' of the set, also responsible for the overall form. Assembled set 38 cm (h). Collection: Alessi.

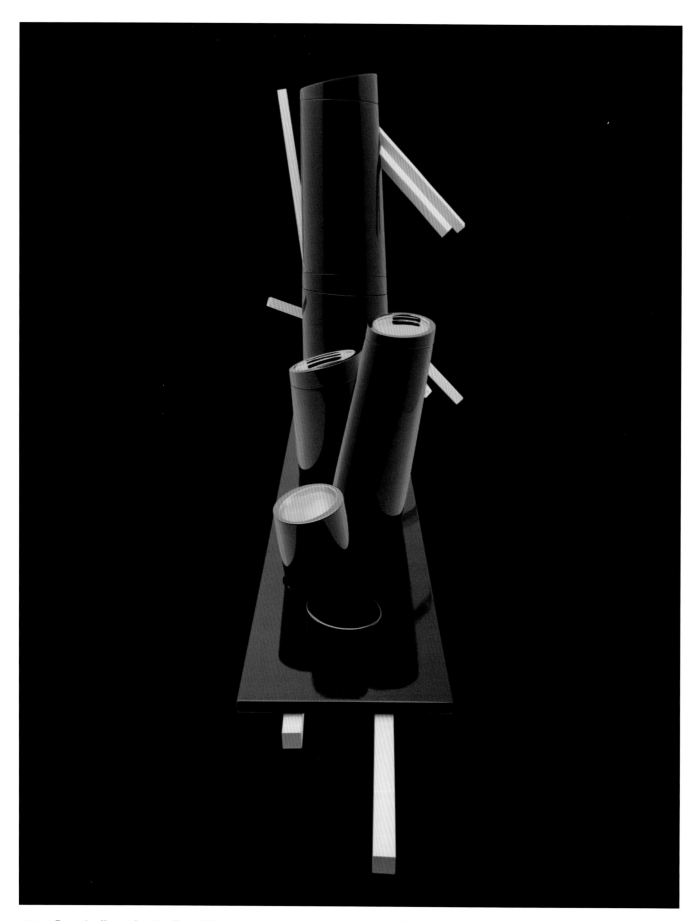

PLATE 84 Tea and coffee set from the 'Tea & Coffee Towers' series, designed by Denton Corker Marshall in Melbourne, Australia, in 2003 for Alessi. Sterling silver plated with black chrome, handles and spouts with yellow thermoplastic resin coating. While this photograph shows individual components ready for use, this strongly architectonic set is intended to be stored as a tower on one end of the tray. As a tower on the tray 87.5 cm (h). Collection: Powerhouse Museum, Sydney.

Photo by Carlo Lavatori courtesy of Alessi.

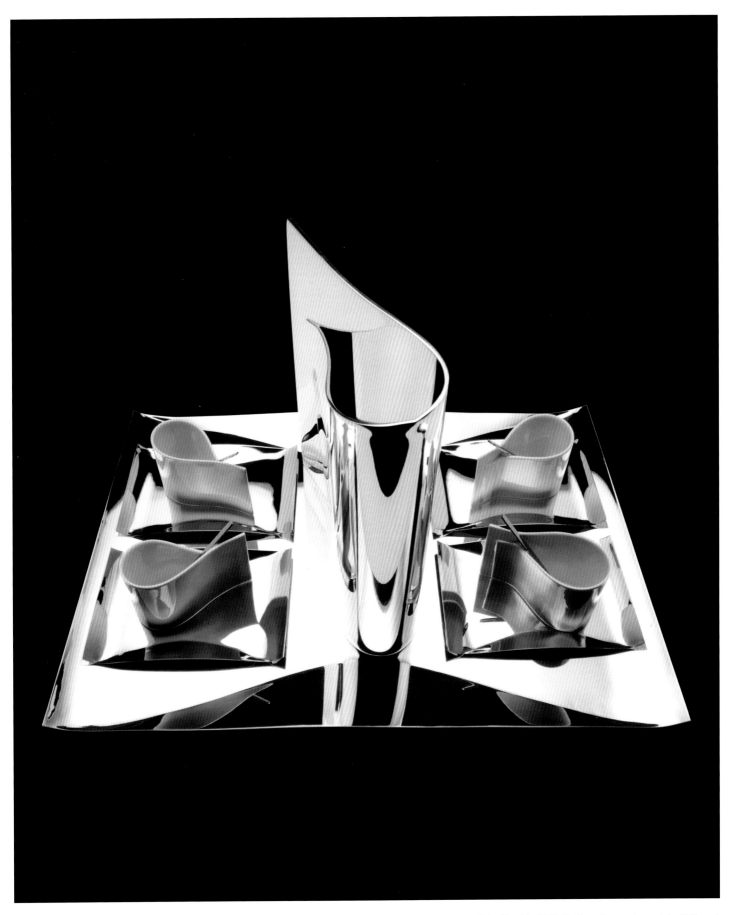

PLATE 85 Coffee set from the 'Tea & Coffee Towers' series, designed by Massimiliano Fuksas and Doriana O Mandrelli for Alessi in 2003. Sterling silver and porcelain. Coffeepot 24 cm (h). Collection: Alessi.

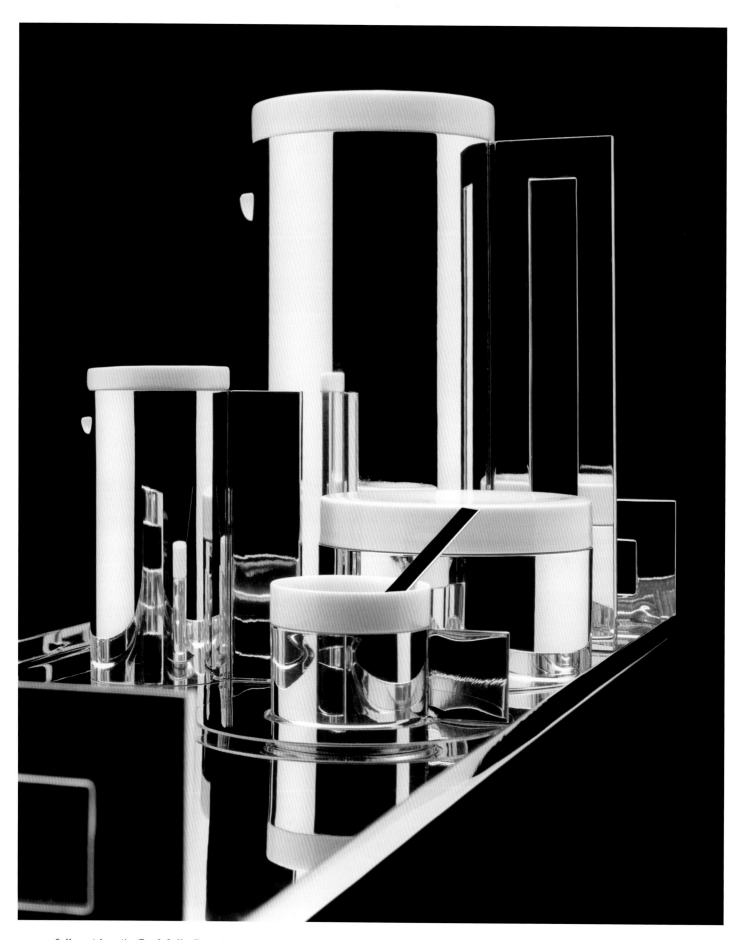

PLATE 86 Coffee set from the 'Tea & Coffee Towers' series, designed by Dominique Perrault in France for Alessi in 2003. Comprises coffeepot, milk jug, sugar bowl, six cups and tray, made in sterling silver with porcelain interiors. Coffeepot: 21cm (h). Collection: Alessi.

Photo by Carlo Lavatori courtesy of Alessi.

PLATE 87 Tea and coffee set from the 'Tea & Coffee Towers' series, designed by David Chipperfield in England for Alessi in 2003. Asymmetrical and fluid, the pots evoke the character of silver as a melting material. The necks, coated with bands of thermoplastic resin, replace the handles. Milk jug and sugar bowl are made in ceramic. Coffeepot: 22.5 cm (h). Collection: Alessi.

Photo by Carlo Lavatori courtesy of Alessi.

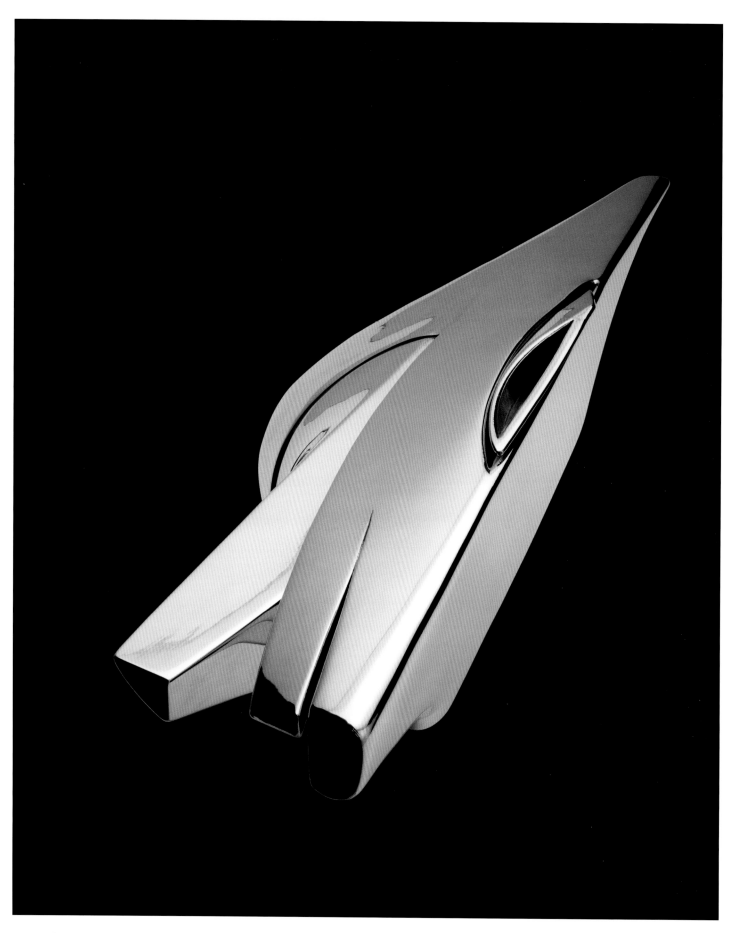

PLATE 88   Tea set from the 'Tea & Coffee Towers' series, designed by Thom Mayne of Morphosis (USA) for Alessi in 2003. When assembled, the double-walled teapot with filter and a milk jug form a distinctive sculpture. Collection: Alessi.

Photo by Carlo Lavatori courtesy of Alessi.

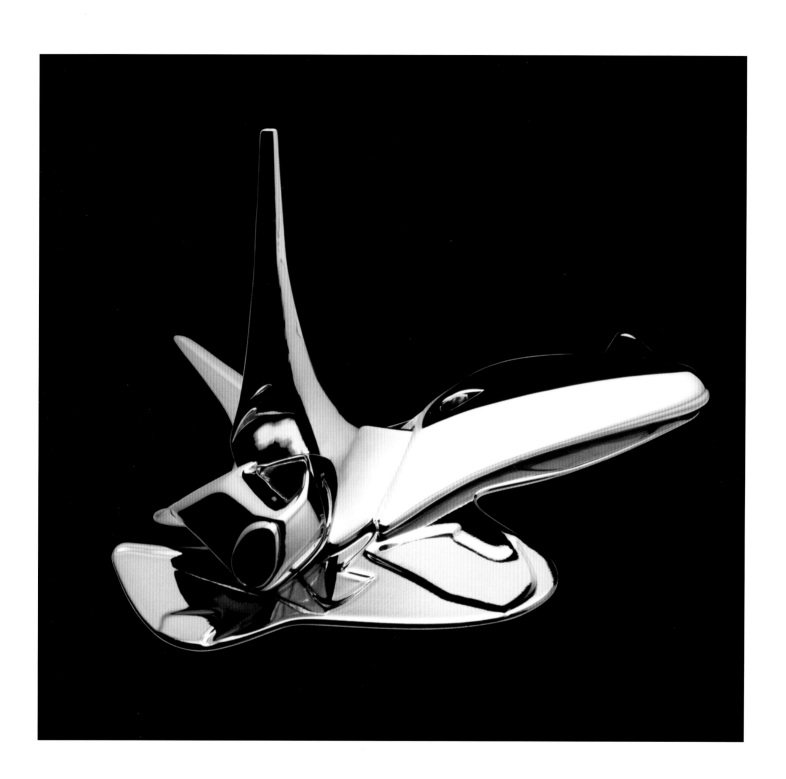

PLATE 89 Tea and coffee set from the 'Tea & Coffee Towers' series, designed by Zaha Hadid in London for Alessi in 2003. This is a table sculpture that splits into five elements: teapot (wide, flat shape), coffeepot (tall, vertical part), milk jug, sugar bowl and tray. Collection: Alessi.

Photo by Carlo Lavatori courtesy of Alessi.

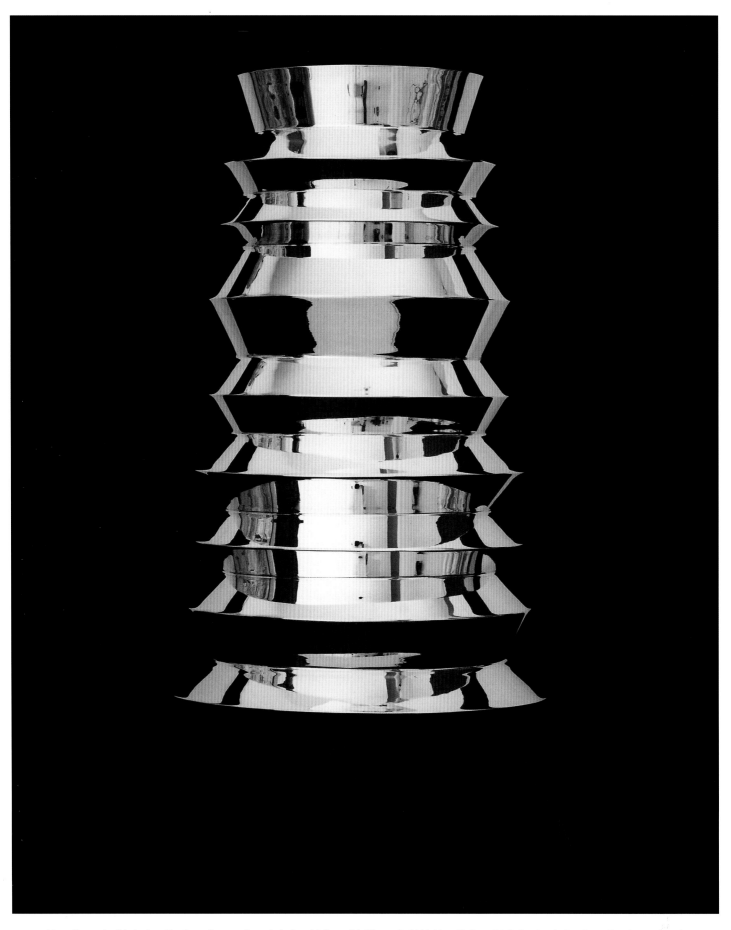

PLATE 90 Vase, 'Sennacherib', designed by Ettore Sottsass Jr, made by Rossi & Arcandi in Vicenza in 2002. Vase 52.5.cm (h). Collection: Gallery Paolo Curti/Annamaria Gambuzzi & Co, Milan and Gallery Bruno Bischofberger, Zurich.

Photo courtesy of Paolo Curti, Milan.

PLATE 91 Fruit stand, 'Ziusudra', designed by Ettore Sottsass Jr, made by Rossi & Arcandi in Vicenza in 2002. Stand 40 cm (h). Collection: Gallery Paolo Curti/Annamaria Gambuzzi & Co, Milan and Gallery Bruno Bischofberger, Zurich.

Photo courtesy of Paolo Curti, Milan.

PLATE 92 Fruit stand, 'Shalmaneser III', designed by Ettore Sottsass Jr, made by Rossi & Arcandi in Vicenza in 2002. Stand 15 cm (h). Collection: Gallery Paolo Curti/Annamaria Gambuzzi & Co, Milan and Gallery Bruno Bischofberger, Zurich.

Photo courtesy of Paolo Curti, Milan.

Further reading

A Colonetti et al, *Gabriele De Vecchi*, Edizioni L'Archivolto, Milan, 1995.

E B Gentili, *Cleto Munari, Dandy design*, exhibition catalogue for Scuderie di Palazzo Reale, Napoli, Electa, Naples, 1997.

T F Giacobone (ed), *Italian silverware of the 20th century: from decorative arts to design*, Electa, Milan, 1993.

T F Giacobone (ed), *La lingua degli specchi: l'atelier De Vecchi 50 anni di storia nell'argento*, Electa, Milan, 1997.

E Marelli, *Lino Sabattini: suggestione e funzione/intimations and craftsmanship*, Edizioni Metron, 1997.

A Mendini (ed), *Tea & coffee towers*, Mondadori Electa, Milan, 2003.

A B Oliva, *La figura delle cose: Cleto Munari in Castel Sant' Angelo*, Electa, Naples, 1999.

B Radice, *Memphis*, Thames & Hudson, New York, 1995.

Tea & coffee piazza, Officina Alessi, Shakespeare & Co, Brescia (Italy), 1985.

The work of the silversmith's studio, San Lorenzo, Milano 1970–1995, exhibition catalogue for the Victoria and Albert Museum, Electa, Milan, 1995.

Acknowledgments

This publication and exhibition celebrate the cooperation between the Powerhouse Museum, Museo per gli Argenti Contemporanei, Museo Alessi and several Italian studios and firms that have generously lent their objects and photographic material and provided advice and information. The production of this book in particular would have not been possible without the assistance provided from Italy by Dr Giorgio Forni (MAC), Giacomo and Matteo De Vecchi, Olga Finzi Baldi, Daniele Brandolin and Dr Diego Fantinelli (Cleto Munari), Dr E Paolo Moroni (Sawaya & Moroni), Dr Gianfranco Pampaloni (Pampaloni Grandi Argenti), Dr Alberto Bianci Albrici (Memphis SRL), Marina Ruggieri (Gemma Gioielli/Fratelli Filippini), Dr Alberto Vallé (Vallé Mario SNC) and Dr Paolo Curti (Gallery Paolo Curti/Annamaria Gambuzzi). Above all I would like to thank San Lorenzo's Dr Ciro Cacchione and Francesca Appiani, Curator, Museo Alessi, assisted by Antonella De Martino, for their exceptional support and patient collaboration.

I also wish to acknowledge the unfailing local support, recieved throughout the project from Ilaria Cornaggia Medici Logi (Silver Puzzle) and Dr Gerlando Butti, Vice Consul and Director of the Italian Institute of Culture in Sydney. I am grateful to Benedetta Calzavara for her excellent research assistance, and to my colleagues Dr Grace Cochrane and Anne Watson and also Judith O'Callaghan for reading and commenting on the manuscript. Finally, my thanks go to text editor Sue Wagner, designer Peter Thorn and Powerhouse staff Lindie Ward, Gara Baldwin, Ryan Hernandez, Anne Slam and Julie Donaldson for their contributions to the publication.

In writing this book, I am indebted to information published in *Design in Italy, 1870s to the present* by Penny Sparke (1988).

About the author

Eva Czernis-Ryl is a curator of decorative arts and design at the Powerhouse Museum. Exhibitions she has curated include *Irish gold and silver*, *Australian gold & silver 1851–1900* and *Treasures from the Kremlin: the world of Fabergé*. She has written and lectured widely on aspects of both historical and contemporary decorative arts in specialist journals both in Australia and overseas. Eva was the content editor and contributing author of the exhibition book *Australian gold & silver 1851–1900* (Powerhouse Publishing, 1995) and a contributing author to *A material world: fibre, colour and pattern* (Powerhouse Publishing, 1990), *Decorative arts and design from the Powerhouse Museum* (Powerhouse Publishing, 1991), and *Heritage, the national women's art book* (Craftsman House, 1995).

About the Powerhouse Museum

The Powerhouse Museum is Australia's largest museum. Part of the Museum of Applied Arts and Sciences established in 1880, the Powerhouse Museum was purpose-built in 1988 in and around a disused power station. Its collection spans decorative arts, design, science, technology and social history, which encompasses Australian and international, and historical and contemporary material culture. The Powerhouse Museum has a reputation for excellence in collecting, preserving and presenting aspects of world cultures for present and future generations.

The Museum's collection includes over 100,000 decorative arts and design objects. It began acquiring silver objects a few years after its collecting history began with the 1879 Sydney International Exhibition. Although today, Australian colonial gold and silver and contemporary Australian hollow ware are the best known components of the decorative metalwork collection, international silverware also features prominently with significant examples of Italian production, both historical and contemporary.

Index of designers and manufacturers